Also by Larry Lain

London for Families
London for Lovers

Other Interlink Titles of Interest

The Cafés of Paris
Edible France: A Traveler's Guide
Food in Five Languages
The Independent Walker's Guide to France
Old Provence
A Shopper's Guide to Paris Fashion
A Traveller's History of France
A Traveller's History of Paris
A Traveller's Wine Guide to France
Vacation Rentals in Europe: A Guide
Wild France

Paris for Families

by Larry Lain

illustrations by Michael Lain

Interlink Books

An imprint of Interlink Publishing Group, Inc.
New York • Northampton

First published 2001 by

INTERLINK BOOKS
An imprint of Interlink Publishing Group, Inc.
99 Seventh Avenue • Brooklyn, New York 11215 and
46 Crosby Street • Northampton, Massachusetts 01060
www.interlinkbooks.com

Library of Congress Cataloging-in-Publication Data

Lain, Larry, 1947–
    Paris for families / by Larry Lain
        p.   cm.
    ISBN 1-56656-360-7 (pbk.)
    1. Paris (France) Guidebooks.   2. Families--Travel--France--
-Paris Guidebooks.   I. Lain, Michael.   II. Title.
DA679.L245   1999
914.2104'859--dc21   99-41374
                                                              CIP

Printed and bound in Canada

To request our complete 48-page full-color catalog,
please call us toll free at **1-800-238-LINK**, visit our
website at **www.interlinkbooks.com**, or write to
Interlink Publishing
46 Crosby Street, Northampton, MA 01060

e-mail: sales@interlinkbooks.com

Contents

Acknowledgements

How do you adequately thank the people who have been at the very root of a project? I could write an entire book about the helpfulness and kindness of each of these good people and not do them justice. I'll just say that without each of them, this book could never have come to be. All I can do is say Thanks, and assure readers that if any mistakes have somehow slipped through, they are mine, not those of the fine folks named here.

Since this is a family book, it's appropriate to thank first of all my favorite travelling companions, my family: My wife, friend, and editor Barb Lain; my son and illustrator Michael Lain and his wife Beth Croghan. (Mike adds his own acknowledgement to Beth "...for helping me get through drawing these stupid things. She did everything but draw them for me.")

Also to Rik and Elizabeth Lain Schell, and Doug and Sunnie Johnson Lain—and Neal, first of a new generation of Lain travellers.

Susan Stavenhagen has been most generous with her advice and extensive knowledge of Paris, and with helping my untrained tongue wrap itself around the language, and Maureen O'Meara has been a big help in straightening out my efforts at translation. I must also thank Pat Oudet of Rendez-Vous Parisien for her helpfulness and generosity, and Lou Jerome and Michael Kremer for their first-hand advice and wealth of ideas.

To all of you, *Merci Beaucoup!*

For the latest updates to *Paris for Families*, check our page on the Web at:

www.interlinkbooks.com/parisforfamilies.html

Introduction

Ah, Paris—a place that has more evocative names and phrases and song titles attached to it than any other city in the world. The City of Lights. April in Paris. Gay "Paree." I Love Paris in the Springtime.... The list could be quite a long one. There must be a reason for it, and visitors will find many reasons during their first hour in this city. Paris is beautiful. Paris is romantic. Paris is throbbing with activity and excitement. And apparently you've already thought of that, or at least been entranced by some of those evocative phrases, or you wouldn't have taken this book off the shelf.

So you're thinking of taking your family to Paris? Excellent choice! Not only is Paris the City of Lovers, it's perfect for families: lots of exciting things to do, so many wonderful things to see—and the food is reputed to be pretty good, too.

Paris is large and it's very old, so you can find not only the usual big-city attractions, but also a dizzying array of unique things to see and do. Paris isn't just a destination for art lovers. You'll find the most modern virtual reality games just minutes' walk from places of grisly executions; see quiet lagoons filled with miniature sailboats not far from tunnels filled with millions of ancient bones; discover ornate palaces within sight of the entrance to the cavernous sewers.

Paris is a great destination, too, because it's an accessible city. The center city is small enough to walk across in a couple of hours. One of the world's best metro systems zips you from place to place even faster. Even if you've never been to Paris before, it's a city you can connect with and feel at home in within a very short time.

Many people avoid foreign travel because they don't speak the language. Don't let that deter you. The Parisians' reputation for unfriendliness is a myth: nowhere will you find people more willing to help you overcome the language differences—if you know how. The first time I went to Paris I spoke no more French than an antelope, and I still understand less than the average poodle, but I not only survived—I prospered. With courtesy, respect, and the smallest amount of effort, you and your family can enjoy Paris, even thrive there! This book will show you how.

Traveling has been one of the real highlights of our family years, and this book will share some of the things we've learned about how to do it—and sometimes how not to—in hopes that your family's travel experiences will be as rich and rewarding as ours have been. The secret is in the planning. Readers of *London for Families* will recognize the approach of this book—when and how to go, what to see (and what to avoid), how to deal with everyday life in a place you may never have visited before, and how to do it in a way that will leave some money in your bank account at the end of the day.

Foreign travel can be intimidating, and the notion of taking a family somewhere you don't know well can be downright scary. It needn't be. This book is your survival kit, your step-by-step guide to the most marvelous family experience you can imagine.

Time passes too quickly. The trips we took together, the fun we had together, the things we saw together… these things are favorite topics of conversation every time the Lains are together. We're so glad we didn't put off our trips "until there's more time" or "until we can afford it." We made time, and we found ways to make it affordable. We never spent either our time or our money on anything that brought our family closer than traveling together, sharing the excitement of new sights and new experiences. The aim of this book is to help your family have as much fun as the Lains have had.

Let's go to Paris!

Carousels are everywhere in Paris. This double-decker is at the Hôtel de Ville

Part I:
Getting Ready for Paris

The fun of planning for a great trip is exceeded only by the trip itself. The first eight chapters of *Paris for Families* will help you get ready for the adventure by telling you everything you and your family need to know to thrive in this spectacular city. Find out how to get there as economically as possible, how to get accommodations that are as comfortable as home, and how to adapt quickly to the local money, transportation, and language issues. Then you will be able to live like a local.

By the time you finish this section, you'll be confident that, even if you've never visited Paris before, you and your family will prosper there; you'll have command of the day-to-day details of life in one of the world's greatest cities. The practical and down-to-earth advice in these chapters will help everyone see just how easy a trip like this can be. You don't want to worry over little details—you want to focus on the excitement of being in Paris with your loved ones. This section shows you how!

1. Planning the Big Adventure

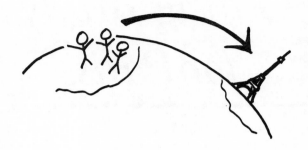

Nothing—absolutely nothing—can top a great family vacation. Everyone has heard horror stories (and many of us can tell them, too—there was this camping trip...) about family holidays gone terribly awry. But when everything goes as planned, there is no better experience. Going to new places together, seeing things in person that have been just disconnected images on a television or movie screen, gawking your way down streets dripping with history: These are the elements of years' worth of dinner-table conversations and experiences that bond you forever.

Our family has had memorable vacations as simple as spending a weekend exploring corners of our hometown we hadn't seen before, or just a few days in a nearby big city. But for a spectacular, truly memorable immersion experience, nothing can top a trip abroad.

The Lains are not, sad to say, wealthy, so our trips have taken careful planning and economizing, and we've discovered—very much to our surprise—that the need to plan and watch our budget have actually made our trips more fun. It has made us learn more about our destination before we go, so we can make the best use of our time and money, and it has forced us to practice the same kind of economy when we travel as we practice at home; indeed, the same kind of economy practiced by the people who actually live in the place we plan to visit: to Live Like a Local.

If you would like to have the same sort of memorable trips our family has been lucky enough to enjoy, this book is for you.

And Paris is the perfect place for your trip.

Of all the mountains, all the oceans, all the great cities of the world, no one place has been written about, sung about, celebrated in every possible way more than Paris. Everybody knows about the Eiffel Tower, Notre Dame Cathedral, the Louvre, Napoleon, and the cafés of the Left Bank. But there are magnificent attractions for every member of your family in Paris.

What about some of the world's creepiest catacombs, stacked high with bones? Or a magnificent museum of dolls? A vast science museum? There's a 2,000-year-old Roman arena where you can stand in the ring and gaze up at exactly the last sight many a gladiator ever saw. You can make an afternoon disappear at a museum of magic. You've probably been to a flea market, but what about a bird market? And what kid can resist the most breathtaking tour in Europe: the Paris Sewers?

Paris for Families is your guide for the most memorable family holiday of your life. It is everything you need to know about making the most of your money, finding a home away from home in the city, and putting together an itinerary that's both practical and fun. Even if you've never been to Paris before and don't speak a word of French, you can thrive in this city, making memories that will be part of your life forever.

Lone travelers or flexible couples can be spontaneous on a trip like this, but if you're traveling with a family, more planning is a must. The rule is simple: The stamina of the person who tires most quickly sets the benchmark for the group. A child (or parent!) who is overly tired or hungry gets crabby, and that can soon spoil the day for everyone in the group. *Paris for Families* will help you decide when and how to go and suggest varied, practical itineraries for families of all sorts. Most important, the book will show you how to organize a trip like this, one where everybody likes everybody else even more at the end than they did at the beginning! Planning is the key.

Here in the first chapter, let's deal with two of the most common planning questions.

When Should We Go?

Well, as soon as possible, actually. The kids aren't getting any younger. In fact, this was the reasoning that got the Lain family in gear. We decided that if we waited until we thought we had enough time and money, we might be able to travel with our grandchildren. But that's not answering your question.

We can look at the question in two ways. The first is, "How old should our kids be to benefit from a trip like this?" It depends on your children. Once they're of school age, the experience will be something they can take back to the classroom and that will give them a broader context of the world to put all their studies in. In *London for Families* we suggested that, generally speaking, children younger than age 10 would probably get less out of the trip than older ones—they often haven't seen enough of their own part of the world to benefit greatly from spending time in somebody else's. As a rule of thumb, that's probably still a reasonable way to look at it. But we've heard from many readers of the London book whose younger children also got a lot out of that trip. You know your kids best.

But we were stumped by a question from one reader who wanted to know what we thought her 18-month-old would enjoy in London. That, it seems to me, is pushing it.

The question can also be read as "What's the best time of year for us to go to Paris?" There are no bad times to visit Paris.

Summer or winter, I've found Paris beautiful and exciting. You'll find advantages to avoiding the summertime, if you can: crowds are smaller, lines are shorter, prices are lower. If you can take advantage of a school holiday in the late fall or early spring, that might be ideal. But be aware that many attractions may close an hour or two earlier or might be open fewer days each week than you'd find in the summertime.

August is the traditional month for Parisians to take their summer holidays, so visitors have typically avoided the city then. While that is no longer as true as it once was, some hotels still offer "low season" rates during that time. The disadvantage is that some hotels, restaurants, and bistros close entirely then. But virtually all the attractions a family is traveling to Paris to see will be open; few families we know visit Michelin-starred restaurants or spend their days sipping espresso outside their neighborhood café, so August is no real impediment to a family visit.

Go when you can. Hotel prices and demand peak in May, June and July, and around Christmas and New Year's. But if you're traveling with kids, you have to work around their school holidays and do the best you can. You don't need a whole month to create a great vacation. Paris can be a getaway over a long weekend for Europeans, although a stay of at least six or seven days makes more sense for visitors from Asia or the Americas.

Don't worry too much about the weather. Heck, there's weather everywhere, and it will make a difference in your trip only if you let it. Sure, late spring and early autumn are ideal with their warm days and cool nights. But midsummer days warmer than 85 degrees Fahrenheit (29 Celsius) are less common than in Mediterranean countries, and daytime midwinter temperatures usually fall no lower than 35-40 degrees (2-5 °C). Heavy snowfalls are very rare and if it rains, carry an umbrella. Attitude is everything!

How Much Will It Cost?

There's no good answer to this question. Every family's needs and expectations are different. But this much is true: You don't have to rob your pension plan, re-mortgage your home, or sell your youngest child to afford it. Most of your costs can be controlled, and in most cases can be limited to what you'd spend at home for the same thing. Take comfort in this fact: More than 2 million people live in Paris. Hardly any of them are millionaires. If ordinary people like you can survive in Paris all year round, you can do it for a week or two.

Chapter 20 will provide some worksheets for you to plan your budget more carefully, but here's a quick guide to Budget Basics.

Costs You Can't Control

For the most part, you have only limited control over how much money it will take to actually get your family to Paris. It really depends mostly on where you're coming from. If your home is in Chicago or Brisbane, you'll have to fly; there is no other choice. From London or Frankfurt you can also take a train or coach, or just drive there. (Better put your car on a ferry or Le Shuttle if you're driving from London!) From Chartres you could probably bicycle.

This book will help you capture the best bargains

Aside from those choices for travelers from Europe, you're stuck with paying whatever it takes. Chapter 3 has some practical advice for minimizing those costs (for example, flying in the winter can cost less than half of summer fares) but for non-Europeans, transportation might well account for half their vacation budget, no matter what they do.

Costs You Can Control

You may be stuck with whatever the airlines or railway decides to charge you for getting to Paris, but once you're there, you have much more flexibility. The easiest and most effective approach is to manage your budget by figuring costs per person/per day. It's a formula that lets you both plan and keep track of your expenses easily. While later chapters will go into much greater detail about each category, this is a good place for an overview.

Accommodations: Most travelers pay much more than they have to for lodging, and end up in an atmosphere that is anything but homey. One secret to an affordable vacation, though, is to rent an apartment. Short-stay apartments abound in Paris. On the last visit I took to Paris to tie up loose ends for this book, I stayed in a spacious studio apartment, easily large enough to be comfortable for three, even four people, located in the heart of the city, for about 425F (€65 or $77 as this is written) per night. I was alone (My wife had to work, darn it!) but if Barb had been free to come, sharing the apartment would have made that price less than 215F each (€33 or $39 per person/per day). Two parents and two children in the same apartment would have paid a little higher rate, but not more than a total of about 500F (about €19 or $23 per person/per day). And it's perfectly possible to find even cheaper accommodations. Chapter 2 will tell you everything you need to know about finding an apartment (or an inexpensive hotel for shorter stays) in Paris. The bottom line: A realistic minimum for accommodations for a family of four can be set at 100F to 150F per person/per day (€15-23 or $18-27). While it's certainly possible to find a hotel room in Paris with a daily rate of more than your annual salary, a reasonable maximum for a family of four might be 200F to 250F per person/per day (€30-38 or $36-46). And that's more than the Lains would be willing to pay. We'd search further.

The PP/PD cost might be a bit higher for two or three people, but even less for five (as it was with us) or more people. As you'll see in the next section, renting an apartment saves you money in other ways, too.

Food: No matter where you are, you'll have to eat—the kids will make sure of that! So this is a category of expenses that you'll have whether you take your family to Paris or not. So decide: Would you rather be sitting in your kitchen eating a sandwich tonight, or eating the same sandwich while sitting along the River Seine? Easy choice! If you can afford to buy food at home, you can afford to eat in Paris. One big advantage to renting a Parisian apartment is the fact that you can cook for yourselves sometimes. Hotel dwellers have no choice—every meal must be eaten in a restaurant, and that can get expensive. In an apartment, you can prepare some meals at home for a fraction of what you'd pay even in a modest neighborhood bistro. Chapter 5 provides a short course on eating well in Paris, but here's the bottom line: A realistic minimum, assuming that you will eat some meals in your apartment each day, is 100-150F per person/per day (€15-23 or $18-27), perhaps less, including an occasional snack, and dinners in some lovely restaurants. In Paris a family can easily spend more money on food in a week than they might on a new car. But it's not necessary. A comfortable maximum of 200 to 300F per person/per day (€30-46 or $36-55) allows enough food to fill even growing teenagers. Oh, it will take more money if you plan to dine in plush restaurants two meals a day, but it's easy to economize without a shred of sacrifice.

Attractions and Admissions: Paris has countless wonderful things to see and do that are completely free. Most major museums have special rates for students and many charge nothing at all for children under 18. You can also invest in the *Carte Musées et Monuments* if many of the things it covers are on your "to-do" list. Prices vary a great deal and every family looks for different things: If the ride to the top of the Eiffel Tower is pricey at more than 60F (€9 or $11), a walk along the Seine is always free; some days will be more expensive than others. The bottom line: A realistic minimum is 50F per person/per day, although it's easy to spend less. If you're averaging 100F per person/per day, you are being far too relentless and single-minded a tourist and should relax a little!

Shopping: No one but you can estimate this category with any hope of accuracy. Some families begin buying as soon as they get off the plane, and their credit card companies know them on a first-name basis. Other families (ours among them, usually) would rather visit an extra museum than an extra department store. Our favorite souvenirs have always been our photographs, our travel journals, and, usually, inexpensive, local items. But everybody will want to pick out some souvenirs to take home. One solution that usually works well is to give the kids a fixed amount like 250F (€38 or $46) each for shopping; more than that has to come out of their own money. But once you've given them the money, let them pick out what they like. Kids often buy what, to adults, seem like trivial things. Maybe you wouldn't be caught dead buying one of those ubiquitous plastic models of the Eiffel Tower (although street vendors must sell them by the billion), but there's no accounting for what kids like. Let them spend 10F on one, or on yet another tee-shirt they'll outgrow in three months, or on whatever will give them something to show their friends when they get home. So what's the bottom line here? A reasonable minimum might be 25F a day. A maximum? Well, how much have you got?

Paris for Families

Local Transportation: Paris is a very walkable city, but sometimes distances are too great, time too limited, or feet too sore for a leisurely stroll. Forget taxis, for the most part. They're an unnecessary expense. Besides, Paris has one of the world's most efficient and easiest-to-use Metro systems. (That's subway for Americans, the underground for the British). You'll find Metro stations within a few minutes' walk of everywhere you want to go, and the system, which is explained in detail in Chapter 6, is simple for everyone in the family to master your first day in the city. Buses, too, are convenient and easy to use, even for someone who doesn't speak a word of French. Single-ride tickets are not inexpensive—about 8F (€1.2 or $1.45—but there are very inexpensive ways to use the system by purchasing special passes or tickets in blocks of 10. All that is covered in Chapter 6. Right now, we're setting a budget. Let's allow 20F per person/per day for this.

Let's add it up; here's a perfectly reasonable per person/per day breakdown for a family trip to Paris:

Lodging	100 to 250F
Food	100 to 300F
Sightseeing	50 to 80F
Shopping	25 to 50F
Transportation	20 to 30F
The Bottom Line	**295 to 410F per person/per day**

That's right: Once you get to Paris, you really can get along on roughly 300F to 400F per person/per day—that's €46-61 or $55-73. And that's for everything: accommodations, food, and sightseeing. It's possible to spend more... a lot more! But if you economize a bit, you really can afford the sort of family trip you must have been fantasizing about when you picked up this book. You won't even wind up living in a Left Bank garret like some impoverished *La Boheme* artist. It's just a matter of living the way you do at home—except your temporary home is one of the most fabulous cities on Earth. And if you do have more money to spend, well, *c'est magnifique!*

Planning is the Key

One or two people can travel on whim, going when and where their impulses and budgets take them; with a family, you have to be much less spontaneous. At the same time, overplanning is deadly. You can't foresee everything that might happen, you can't imagine what other neat things you might discover, and you do not want to have everything so tightly programmed that everyone spends a week or two rushing around like they are about to miss the last train to Utopia. Most of all, you want to give yourself the time and opportunity to be surprised. Look, you couldn't see all of Paris in a year, so there's no point in trying to do it in a week. Paris isn't going anywhere: It will still be there if you want it again later. Relax!

The important thing is that everybody takes part in the planning, from Mom and Dad down to the youngest member of

Everyone should get their first choice

the family—unless you're taking an 18-month-old, perhaps. (Then, I guess, you e-mail me for advice...) Everyone should read chapters 10 through 17 of this book, and use Chapter 18 to decide what they want to see and what they don't. Rule No. 1: Everyone gets his or her first choice. Rule No. 2: Everyone is tolerant of everyone else's first choice.

Nothing—not even money—is more important to a successful vacation than attitude... especially a vacation to another country, another culture, where so much is unfamiliar. Everyone needs to agree in advance to work hard at being cheerful and relaxed, even when they're hungry or thirsty or tired. That's so much easier to do if all members of the family feel they had a significant role in planning such a complicated trip.

That's really what this book is about. If your family can have the same sort of fun and forge the same sorts of lasting bonds the Lains did, you'll make memories that will be part of your family gatherings for the rest of your lives. And your humble (well, not very humble) author will be very happy.

Nothing in Paris is more popular than its cafés. The Café des Phares is at the Place de la Bastille

Recommendations

✔ Avoid the busiest times of year for the most economical trip.

✔ Stay long enough to relax. One day for every hour or two of one-way travel time is close to minimum.

✔ Make sure every member of the family takes part in the planning. Everyone will be more tolerant and agreeable if his or her ideas are taken seriously.

✔ Budget all your expenses except travel on a per person/per day basis.

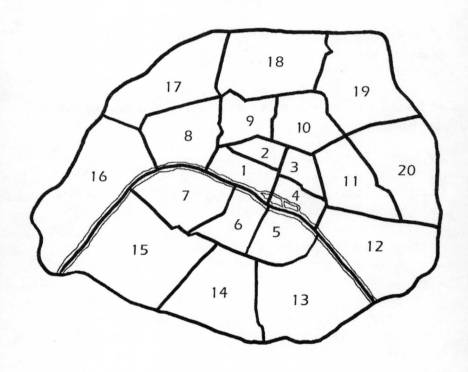

Paris Arrondissements

2. Coming Home to Paris

If you're going to pull off a major family expedition like a trip to Paris, you'll have two major expenses—travel and lodging. Unless you're coming from Western Europe, travel will be the biggest item. Chapter 3 will deal with actually getting to Paris, and will offer tips for doing it economically.

The process of arranging travel, though, is a relatively simple one, done in your own country and speaking your own language. For people who have not traveled widely, it's much more intimidating to make arrangements on somebody else's turf, perhaps in a language in which they have little—or No!— fluency. *That* keeps more people at home than the cost of airfare.

This chapter will help your make those arrangements with ease, however, and will show you how to reduce the cost of accommodations, your second biggest expense, to a fraction of what less savvy travelers pay. And best of all, it will help you *Live Like a Local*, getting far closer to the Parisian way of life than the usual visitor. This should be your object, after all, on a *family* trip. You take your kids on a trip like this (at considerable cost and inconvenience) so they can have the broadening experience of another culture, another way of doing things.

The most magical part of travel is being, as much as you can, *a part of* a place, not *apart from* it.

Paris Hotels

The easiest way of arranging somewhere to stay is to pick up the phone and telephone the reservations number of a major international chain and ask them to give you a room in their Paris hotel. If you have more money in life than you need, go ahead and do that. If, though, you're like most of us and trying to get the most value out of every bit of your money, that's an approach that makes no more sense than sending cash gifts to rich people you don't know.

Paris has some spectacular hotels. I know because I've peeked inside some of them, feeling like an intruder. No, a luxurious hotel with a weekly room rate of more money than the annual budget of a developing nation is not a place the Lain family is likely to stay. I look and admire, then return again to the Paris streets, only a bit ruefully. There are better places for us.

Luxury hotels charge for a lot of things a family doesn't want or need. You won't use their conference facilities, their 24-hour secretarial service, their grand ballroom, their masseuse, or, probably, their health club or their Michelin-starred restaurant. All you'll do with their enormous marble and crystal lobby is walk through it on the way to the elevator. But you're paying for all this and more in a fancy hotel. Do you really *need* a maid to come in and turn down the covers of your bed at night?

If you're watching your budget, you can do better. Much better.

Types of Hotels

When you look at Paris maps and guidebooks, you see hotels all over the place. But not all hotels offer accommodations.

The word *hotel* has many meanings. It might be a mansion or an elegant private residence or an important building. The *Hôtel de Ville* is the "city hall" of a city. The chief hospital of a French city is very often called the *Hôtel Dieu*.

Now that we have that bit of confusion out of the way, we'll talk only about the sort of hotel where you can get a room for the night.

French hotels are graded on a system of stars that indicate the amenities each offers; the more stars, the higher the price. Very basic hotels will have only *one star*, will be unlikely to have elevators or provide toilets in many rooms. In such hotels, shared facilities like toilets and bath or shower rooms each serve two or three sleeping rooms. *Two-star* hotels will usually have toilet and bath facilities in most rooms; some may have elevators. *Three-star* hotels will have more amenities, private baths in all rooms, and those rooms will be larger. When you get to *four-star* hotels, you'll have more spacious rooms and hotels with many public facilities. The highest grade is *four-star luxe*, the true luxury hotels, where the Lains feel like interlopers.

Prices will vary quite a bit, even within each category, by location, amenities, and the surrounding competition, but broadly, here's what you can expect from hotel prices per night based on a double room. There usually will be an extra charge for each additional person of 5-10F. These are average prices. It's possible to find hotels in each category that fall outside the range on either the high or low end.

★	300-500F (€46-76 or $54-91)
★★	400-700F (€61-107 or $72-127)
★★★	600-1000F (€92-153 or $109-182)
★★★★	900-1500F (€137-229 or $163-272)
★★★★L	1500-3500F (€229-534 or $272-636)

For stays of less than a week, a hotel is probably the best option, even for a family, but unless you make a habit of giving away money to strangers, there's no reason to get more hotel than you need. Many tourists automatically gravitate to three- and four-star hotels because they're a safe choice, travel agents have lists of them, and they may be part of familiar chains. But part of what you're buying in the room rate is their international marketing, their familiar name, and the lady who comes around turning down your covers at bedtime. Families on a budget don't need those things.

How much time do you intend to spend in your room? Probably not a lot. Sleeping, relaxing a bit before going out to dinner and before bedtime. For most people, that's about it. You're not making a trip like this to sit in your room. It's silly to buy more stars than you need. If it's the only way to afford a trip like this, a family of three can even manage in a small room with a bed for the adults and room on the floor for the child to camp out at night.

Minimizing Your Hotel Bill

As Chapter 1 suggested, the best way of keeping track of your costs, managing your budget, and comparing facilities is to calculate what you pay *per person/per day*. On that basis, a luxury hotel could easily cost 800F per person/per day. (€122 or $145) That's an outrageous amount just to sleep. Less than two weeks at that rate comes to more money than my parents paid for the house I grew up in! Of course my kids think I'm so old that my first home was a cave.

The biggest drawbacks to less expensive hotels are that the rooms are often relatively small, and that they might not have private facilities. Still, you can often get what you need in a roundabout way. Even one-stars usually have some rooms with private toilets and showers, and the rates for those rooms may be less than comparable rooms in hotels with more stars. It pays to shop around. You can also often reduce the cost of your room by adopting the money-saving strategies in the sidebar *Paris for Cheapskates* in this chapter.

> ***Tip:*** *When you check in, always ask to see the room before registering. This is common in small European hotels and no one will think it odd. If the room is smaller or different from what you've agreed, ask to see another.*

Following this advice, it should not be unrealistic for you to find—depending on the area and the time of year—a big room at a three-star hotel, or a suite (or two adjacent rooms) at a one-star or inexpensive two-star hotel for less than 800F per night. Per person/per day, that works out to be

3 people at 267F (€41 or $48)
4 people at 200F (€31 or $36)
5 people at 160F (€24 or $29)

That's much more reasonable. If you can manage with just one room, and can find a good-sized one at a one- or two-star hotel for 500F (and it's possible to do better that that!) your cost becomes

3 people at 167F (€25 or $30)
4 people at 125F (€19 or $23)

You don't have to spend a lot on a hotel

More people than that in one of the typically small rooms of hotels in that class might be a little tight, but if you can *find* a big room for that price, grab it—and be sure you ask to see it when you check in.

But there's another strategy that might pay even bigger dividends in space, convenience, and cost.

Renting a Paris Apartment

Unless you have an aunt in Paris you can stay with, the cheapest way to live in Paris is to become a Parisian—rent your own apartment! To families who have never done it, this seems a pretty unlikely thing to do, but take it from the Lains and thousands of other people: For a stay of a week or more, it's very easy and very economical.

Paris is packed with apartments that visitors can rent for a week or less or for six months or more, but they're best for visits of at least a week. You can find them in all parts of town and at all times of the year, and countless numbers of them are located in the inner arrondissements near the attractions you'll want to visit.

Apartments have many wonderful advantages over hotels. First of all, even a small apartment will be larger than even an expensive hotel room. Studio apartments usually have enough room for separate sitting, eating, and sleeping areas, as well as a full bathroom; apartments of one and two bedrooms are more spacious than all but the grandest hotel suites.

Paris for Cheapskates

The most consistent advice hotel managers have whispered over the years has been "Don't pay the rack rate." Hotel prices are always negotiable.

Part of getting the best price for a room is vigilance. In Paris, hotel guests are charged a taxe de séjour of 3–7F per person, per night depending on the number of stars the hotel has. This tax should be included in the rate but sometimes is not in order to make the hotel's rates look a bit lower. Be sure to ask.

An apartment with one or more bedrooms gives everyone a chance for more privacy, something that becomes more desirable as the vacation grows longer. An apartment provides a much more home-like atmosphere, too, with comfortable furniture to sit on, often a stereo or CD player to listen to, and a refrigerator to keep snacks and cold drinks.

The price? Typically in the range of two- or three-star hotels, and often less.

You save money another way, too. Because you can do your own cooking, you spend much less money on meals. A good strategy is to eat breakfast in your apartment before setting out for the day. Have lunch as a break from afternoon

Readers of London for Families will recall how we raved about the breakfasts that were usually included in lower-priced hotels. In Paris? Forget it! Most hotels do include breakfast, but it's nothing like the traditional English fry-up. Most Parisians breakfast on coffee or hot chocolate and croissants or bread with jam. That's what you'll get in most places. Be sure to ask, because occasionally you'll be offered a buffet that will also include cereal and fresh fruit, though never anything like the English artery-clogger. If you decide to pass on the breakfast, ask when you reserve the room for its cost to be deducted from your rate. Most, but not all, hotels will comply— but only if you ask. You can break your fast more cheaply with supplies from the local grocery store.

The really frugal traveler can consider a room without its own toilet or bath facilities. Shared facilities are common in Europe and room prices are markedly lower.

Although it pushes the price a bit higher again, you can ask about a two-room suite at an inexpensive hotel. The cost will be more than a single room, but less than the cost of two rooms. It's often possible to rent two adjacent rooms, one with all the plumbing and one without, for a reasonable price, giving a large family plenty of room to spread out.

The best advice, though, is to talk directly to the manager. If you telephone the hotel during the daytime hours in Paris, you'll be able to speak personally with the person who has the last word on what you'll have to pay. Tell him or her that you're trying to get the best possible price and ask for a reduction. Offering to bring your own towels or linens for extra people in the room might get the usual 5-10F charge waived. Offer to pay in cash. Businesses have to pay credit card companies a fee of 2 to 3 percent of a sale,

sightseeing; you can get inexpensive sandwiches from many bakeries and countless street vendors, and cafés are plentiful. Back at the apartment in the evening you can fix a simple supper while everyone relaxes.

sometimes more. If you pay cash, some hotels will pass that savings on to you. Show flexibility, if you can, on arrival or departure days or on weekend stays. Let the manager know how excited you are to be bringing your family to such a wonderful city. Very few hotel managers will refuse to work with you on the price.

Remember the advice travelers have heard so often: Never pay rack rate.

Consider that for a family of four, the simplest inexpensive café breakfast will cost 50F or more. Lunch of a sandwich, a piece of fruit, and a drink for four people will run close to 200F, and dinner at a café or inexpensive bistro may approach 400F. If you stay in a hotel, that's how you must live. Your family will eat *at least* 650F worth of food a day, every day. That's 4,550F a week—€694 or $827!

If you stay in an apartment and shop at a local market, that 650F might buy enough food to feed your family breakfast and dinner every day all week long. Eating lunches out produces a total of 2,050F for the week, just €313 or $372, well under what you would have spent otherwise. If you want a budget option, this is it!

When you rent an apartment in Paris, all the essentials will be provided: sheets and blankets, towels, dishes, cooking utensils, everything you need to feel just like home. Most apartment managers will meet you at the apartment with the keys, and there is often a security keypad with an entry code that unlocks the outer door. Many apartments are in historic buildings and may not have elevators to upper floors, something to ask about if anyone in your group has a problem with stairs.

One Lain favorite, just by way of example, is a spacious studio apartment, easily large enough for four people, a few blocks from the Pompidou Center. It's on the first floor

(European style—one flight up from the street) of a seventeenth-century building on a narrow street. Its windows overlook a small courtyard that is hidden from the street by a high wall. The apartment has a well-equipped kitchen, microwave oven, dinette for four, several comfortable chairs, a sofa that opens into a double bed, a loveseat that opens into a wide single bed, a bathroom that's larger than the one we have at home, and lots of storage and floor space. There's a bakery next door, a small market across the street, a large grocery store a block away, and a Metro station at the end of the street. The price? About the same as a room in a two-star hotel that has about one-third the space.

This apartment isn't unique by any means. Paris has hundreds of them, scattered in all corners of the city. The next sections will show you just how to find the perfect hotel or apartment for your family's big adventure.

Shopping for Your Paris Home

Finding accommodation in Paris is easy. Countless hotel chains with telephone numbers you can call for free are eager to welcome you to Paris, carry your bags, and turn down your bed at night. At a price that would give an oil baron pause. Your travel agent has a good list of hotels, including many small, inexpensive ones, where rooms are barely big enough for two, much less a family. Apartments? No way!

It would be easy if you could just hang out in Paris for a couple of weeks, inspecting hotels and tracking down apartments. That's probably not an option. That's OK. You can still do the legwork from home and come up with a great temporary home in Paris. All you need are an envelope, a stamp, and a telephone to get started. If you can add a fax machine and a computer connected to the Internet, there's nothing you can't do.

Choosing a Hotel or Apartment

First of all, get in touch with the *Office de Tourisme* in Paris to request its *Paris hotel booklet*. This little guide gives you the essential information about hundreds of Paris lodgings in all parts of the city and in all price ranges. There might be a French Tourist Office in your own country, and if there is, *it* can send you the information. But it's just as fast to contact Paris directly. The address is:

Office de Tourisme
127 Avenue des Champs-Élysées
Paris 75008 France
You can also contact them in three other ways:
Telephone: +33 01 49 52 53 54
Fax: +33 01 49 52 53 00
Web Page: http://www.francetourism.com
When you phone or fax, the +33 is the international telephone code for France. You'll need to first dial your country's international access code (in North America, for instance, it's *011*) followed by *33*, followed by the number. If you're calling from outside France, omit the first *0*. There's no need to be concerned with language at this point. Numerous languages are spoken at the main tourist office and the website is available in several as well.

Armed with information from the book, you can pick out several places that appear to fall into your price range and location. Then telephone the managers! It's not as expensive as you might think, even if you're calling from as far away as the United States or Australia. For no more than the price of a good lunch you can telephone three or four possible hotels or apartments and find out exactly the information you need—much better than *any* guidebook. You can also discuss price with the manager, and find ways to save as much money as possible. In Chapter 20 you'll find a form you can fill out as you talk to the proprietors.

Keep the time difference in mind when you telephone. Paris is one hour earlier than Greenwich Mean Time, and to speak to the manager, you'll almost certainly need to call during daytime business hours in Paris—even if that means it's 3 a.m. where *you* live. It's worth it.

Once you've talked with several people and decided on the place you want to stay, call back again, speak to the manager, and remind him or her of your earlier conversation. Confirm the price (and see if you can get it reduced a bit more) and make the booking.

You will probably be asked for a deposit. Generally a credit card can be used for this, but

---

Getting Your Bearings

Paris is divided into 20 administrative districts called *arrondissements*, with the 1st Arr. in the center and the numbers spiraling out in a clockwise fashion. They have very distinctive characters and each has advantages and disadvantages. The districts south of the River Seine are called the Left Bank: arrondissements 5, 6, 7, 12, 13, 14, 15. The rest is called the Right Bank.

Your best bet is to stay in one of the inner, lower-numbered districts. Prices are a little higher here but you'll spend less time on the Metro and many of the sights you want to see will be within walking distance. *This* is the Paris of your imagination. Here's a summary of the central arrondissements.

1st—Relatively expensive because it's so central. The Louvre, Tuileries, and Palais Royal are here, and some of the grandest hotels, as well as part of the central island, Cité.

2nd—More commercial than residential, home to some of the world's most extravagant shopping. An easy walk from almost everything.

3rd—Much of it is part of the Marais, one of the most unspoiled parts of Paris. Many apartments and cafés. Rather run-down a generation ago, its revitalization has made it a popular place to live. Rents are generally reasonable.

4th—Part of the Marais, the 4th oozes charm. Many apartments and small hotels, some very reasonable. Can be busy and noisy at night. The Pompidou Center and Hotel De Ville are here. Good shopping and great eating.

5th—Heart of the Latin Quarter, so called because the scholars who lived and studied here in medieval times spoke Latin, not French. Fun and busy part of town. Great restaurants

some small hotels, generally one-star, don't accept them. In that case, you will have to have a bank draft in francs or euros prepared by your local bank.

Note this as well: In France, a booking like this is considered a legal contract. If your plans change, the manager is under no obligation to return your deposit and can, in fact, charge you for the full amount of the reservation. You might want to investigate trip cancellation insurance. It's inexpensive and either your travel agent or the agent who handles your household insurance can help you.

and some over-priced touristy ones. Expensive in places, cheap in others. Wide variety of hotels and apartments. The Panthéon and Natural History museums are the big attractions.

6th—Home of the most famous cafés and many nice apartments and hotels, which may be a bit above average in price.

7th—A bit more expensive but great charm: The Eiffel Tower is at your doorstep, along with Invalides, the Orsay, the Rodin, and much else.

8th—Very expensive residential area bordering the Champs-Élysées. This is a status address.

You can also find good close-in accommodation in the Opéra Quarter (9th), Republique (where the 3rd, 10th, and 11th come together), Montparnasse (14th and 15th), and many lovely places in Montmartre (18th). The outer reaches of those arrondissements, though, get rather far from the center. In Montmartre, avoid places within a block or two of the Pigalle and Clichy metros which, although safe, are close to much of Paris's adult entertainment.

Using the Fax as a Tool

Some readers have already found a problem with the truly excellent advice above. I'm not offended: I thought of it, too, the first time I planned a Paris trip. Here it is: *How can I call anybody? I don't speak French!*

One of the biggest reasons people stay at expensive hotels is because they have confidence that they won't need French to get along; someone will speak their language. That's true, but it's also true in most inexpensive hotels as well. Remember that France is the leading tourist destination in the world; the French are quite used to an assortment of other languages, particularly English and often German, Italian, and Spanish, as well as other European languages. Asian languages are less often found but that situation is gradually improving, too.

Parisians do, however, deeply appreciate the efforts of foreigners to acknowledge their language. As Chapter 8 stresses, interactions will almost *always* go more smoothly if you can begin with a few words in French, however poorly. Try beginning a conversation by saying, *Bonjour! Excusez-moi. Je ne parle pas français. Parlez-vous anglais / allemand / italien / espagnol?* (Hello! I'm sorry. I don't speak French. Do you speak English / German / Italian / Spanish?)

If the answer is *non* and you can't make your way in French, you'll have to go on to the next step: Fax.

Nearly every Paris hotel, large and small, has a fax machine, and this is the second-best way of making initial arrangements. A fax to Paris normally costs even less than a phone call because it's faster. You lose the personal contact of conversation, but you gain a lot of flexibility if you have little or no command of French.

When I fax a French hotel I usually write in English, with a French translation at the bottom. There's no point in my trying to pretend that I'm fluent (or even adequate!) in French because I'm not, but the courtesy of writing in French is always appreciated by the recipient. The reply usually comes in English that is invariably better than my French. Chapter 20 includes samples—even in French—that you can adapt and use.

If you have access to the World Wide Web—from home, from work, from your local library, from an "Internet Café"—you can use a free site that will allow you to make pretty accurate translations of documents to and from French, English,

German, Italian, Spanish, and Portuguese. It will also translate web pages in those languages with reasonable accuracy. The address is:

http://babelfish.altavista.com/translate.dyn

Since it's free, there are bound to be drawbacks. The biggest is that it works mostly between English and other languages. To translate between Spanish and French, for example, you would have to translate the Spanish to English, and the resulting English into French. Despite the extra step, literal accuracy is pretty good.

Once you have arranged a booking, put all the details—dates, price, extras, arrangements like a deduction for breakfast, etc.— into a letter or fax and send it. Make sure you include your estimated arrival time to insure that your room will still be there if you arrive after 7 PM. Keep a copy of what you send and request a written confirmation.

Using the Web as a Tool

Using the Web as a translator is only the beginning of its possibilities, however. It's fast becoming the savvy traveler's most important research tool. The Web is the richest vein of information imaginable. From the computer you have access to scores of websites listing thousands of hotels and apartments.

Of course a caveat is in order, here. You *can't* accept everything you see on-line at face value. The same thing applies to books, for that matter (except this one, of course...). Anybody can put up a Web page and say whatever they want. But if the same place is listed on two or more unrelated websites, you can begin to have a bit more confidence. Look for photographs of the property and for endorsements from people who have stayed there. This is especially useful if their e-mail addresses are included so you can write to them directly and make sure the site didn't just put up their good comments and leave out the bad.

The Internet is like a friend who knows the best deals

More than 2,000 Paris hotels and hundreds of apartments are listed on the Web. Many have their own websites, and this is usually great because those are normally the places with the most information and pictures. Their opinions cannot, however, be regarded as unbiased.

You'll also find sites run by booking agencies. These will have listings for all the properties they represent, and they'll often promise discount rates. It's been my experience, though, that the rates I get by contacting the proprietor directly are always at least as good, and usually better, than those offered by an agency.

You will also find more comprehensive lists of hotels and apartments posted as a service, usually carrying advertising. These can be exhaustive in length and exhausting to read through. If you're limiting yourself to a certain class of hotel, a certain size of apartment, and/or a certain area of the city, you can usually sort out the possibilities quickly.

The *World Wide Web Information* section on page 267 in this chapter lists some of the best Paris accommodation websites available. Once you've narrowed down the possibilities, start phoning and faxing. Here are some things to establish:

For a hotel:
Where is the hotel? What's the nearest Metro?
How large is the room?
What kind of bath/toilet facilities are in the room?
What is the charge for extra people?
Are rollaway beds available for extra people?
If we don't use a rollaway or bring our own linens for it, is there a deduction?
Does the room face the street or a courtyard? How quiet is it?
Does the room have a telephone? TV? Alarm clock?
Is breakfast provided? What does it consist of?
If we don't take breakfast, how much will you deduct from our rate?
How far away is the nearest self-service laundry?
What is the best price you can give me, including all taxes?
Is there any way to reduce it further? (like length of stay, weekend specials, etc.)

For an apartment:
What is the address of the apartment? What's the nearest Metro?
How large is the apartment? How many beds?
Describe the building. When was it last refurbished?
Describe the neighborhood. Is it residential, commercial, industrial?
What kind of bath/toilet facilities are in the apartment?
Does the apartment face the street or a courtyard? How quiet is it?
Describe the furnishings and appliances in the apartment.
Describe the cooking facilities in the apartment.
Does the apartment have laundry facilities?
How far away is the nearest self-service laundry? Grocery store? Bakery? Produce market?
How do we pick up the keys?
What is the best price you can give me, including all taxes?
Is there any way to reduce it further? (like length of stay, weekend specials, etc.)

After three or four conversations like this, you can have considerable confidence that you're getting just what your family needs, and at the best price available.

This process is more time consuming that just turning it over to a travel agent or calling a telephone number for an international hotel chain. But frankly, the research is part of the fun, and you learn a lot more about your destination and about what to expect by doing it this way. You'll also end up with nicer facilities and a lower cost. To remind yourself of that, just before everybody goes to bed on your first night in your Paris apartment, go around and turn back the covers of each bed—then ask yourself just how much you would have been willing to pay somebody *else* to do that.

Recommendations

✔ If you're staying for a week or more, rent an apartment. You'll have more space, more privacy, and save money.

✔ Figure your costs on the basis of per person/per day to get the best comparisons.

✔ If you can, use the World Wide Web at a tool for finding the broadest range of accommodations.

✔ Communicate directly with the proprietor of hotels and apartments via phone or fax. It's a key to getting the most information and the best rate.

For the latest updates to Paris for Families, check our
page on the Web at:

www.interlinkbooks.com/parisforfamilies.html

3. The Art of Traveling

S omeday a smart scientist is going to perfect teleportation,
and a grateful world will raise a golden statue a half mile
high to the genius. Maybe that will have happened
between the time this book is written and the time you buy it,
in which case you can skip this chapter. If, alas, teleportation
hasn't become available by the time you're ready to go to Paris,
you'll just have to endure travel the old-fashioned way—
bumping along in the car, rolling along in a train, or being
shoehorned into an airplane seat and shot at improbable speeds
through the sky.

It's worth it to get to Paris.

How much of an inconvenience it will be to get from
wherever you are to Paris depends on where you are! You can
leave Reims after breakfast, travel down the A4, and be in Paris
before the restaurants open for lunch. Drive from Cologne or
London (via ferry or tunnel) and you'll still arrive well before
the dinner hour. But from very much further away, the easy
drive becomes an expedition involving wearying hours on the
road and overnight stops.

Trains offer more relaxation and ease of travel, but even at that, you could end up spending more of your holiday than you'd wish traveling to Paris instead of being there. If you're coming from more than a thousand kilometers away, you'll probably be flying in, something that always has the trappings of a major production.

Traveling by Land

Even if you're coming from the Ile de France region, the area immediately surrounding Paris, you might be better off to leave your automobile at home and take the train. Driving in Paris is, perhaps, less difficult than climbing the 1,652 steps up the Eiffel Tower, but it's no more fun and finding a place to park can take as long. And parking is expensive! Besides that, it is usually quicker to get where you're going inside Paris on the Metro. Unless you know the tricks and secret parking places of the lifelong Parisian, you might enjoy the trip more if you leave the car at home.

Driving

But people do drive into Paris on holiday. If you know of an inexpensive place to park, it's cheaper than trains and planes. Carrying luggage is convenient, you can drive directly to your apartment or hotel, and drivers can set their own timetables. But personally, the idea of a vacation seems to suggest seeking *less* stress, and driving in heavy traffic on unfamiliar streets does not sound like a prescription for stress reduction.

If you must drive, however, try to arrive in Paris at midday, when traffic volume is between the insane peaks of rush hour. Sunday afternoon, too, is usually a good time to arrive.

Keep the kids occupied and quiet in the back seat by making sure each is equipped with books, games, and food. Each child can take his or her own "carry-on bag," just like on an airplane, packed with things to do during the trip.

Stop and let kids walk around and stretch at least every hour or two. If it's convenient, stop at interesting places near the highway for a head start on your sightseeing. Paris is ringed by fabulous cathedrals (for example, at Reims, Chartres, and

Parking can be a real problem in Paris

Rouen), spectacular castles and chateaux (like Compiègne and Chambord), and historic areas (Verdun and the Argonne Forest, for instance).

Trains

Taking the train is much more comfortable than driving. You're faced with no traffic jams on the Périphérique, no flat tires on the motorway, and no parking garages that cost as much per night as your hotel room. When the kids get restless they can get up and walk around, and you never have to stop along the way for everyone to use the toilet. I'd travel by train all the time if I could… but very few trains run from the U.S. Midwest to Paris.

High-speed trains like the TVG or the Eurostar are a practical alternative to flying medium-range distances. Prices are comparable and travel time is about the same, when you take into account the time it takes to travel between the airport and central Paris. Regular trains cost less but take longer.

It's impossible to give information about train travel that's too specific because every national railway system has slightly different rules. Generally speaking, though, shopping for a train ticket is much like shopping for a plane ticket.

Buy your tickets in advance. Special discounts are usually available for advance purchases.

• Discounts are often available for weekend stays.

• Special family fares, or discounts for children, are common.

• Second-class or standard class tickets are better value than first-class tickets. The lower-priced carriages get to the station at the same time as the high-priced cars.

Save money by packing your own meals to take on board. Food is expensive on the train, and usually not very good.

Here, too, kids can take their own carry-on bags. If they have portable radios or hand-held video games, make sure they bring earphones. Most trains require them and *all* your fellow passengers will appreciate it.

Traveling by Air

Most people arrive in Paris by air; the city's two major airports handle 60 million arrivals and departures a year. If you're coming from anywhere outside of Western Europe (and often from within), odds are strong that your first view of Paris will be Charles de Gaulle or Orly airport.

There's no getting around it: Flying a family all the way to Paris from the Americas, Asia, or Africa is expensive, probably half the total cost of the entire vacation. There are tricks to finding the best airfare that experienced travelers know, however, that can cut your ticket prices by one-third or more, and the sidebar in this chapter, *Finding the Fairest Fare*, will tell you all you need to know about that.

Travel Agent or Do It Yourself?

There was a time when, unless you were willing to accept an airline's word that it alone offered the lowest price to a destination (certainly a questionable leap of faith), you *needed* the services of a travel agent. Only with her sophisticated computer software could you sort through the maze of fares and restrictions and have any hope at all of not paying twice as much for your seat as the guy across the aisle from you. Best of all, the agent's services were free! She was paid through commissions from the airline.

Things have changed. You now have access to most of the same computer databases as your travel agent over the World Wide Web. Airlines have reduced or capped commissions to travel agents, forcing many of them to charge customers directly for their services. So why would someone with Internet access bother with going through a travel agent?

The *right* travel agent can still make a difference. If you have a travel agent who has

Finding the Fairest Fare

The tax code of the United States, the decline and fall of the Roman Empire, and the Theory of Relativity—all of these, taken together—are easier to understand than the pricing systems used by the world's airlines. A few, to be sure, do have fare structures of fixed and consistent prices to specific destinations. But more often, passengers will have to thread their ways through a maze of prices and regulations that's harder than learning a foreign language—backwards!

There are tricks to getting the lowest fare, though, and whether you're using a travel agent or striking out on your own over the Web, you'll get a better deal if you know the secrets. These tips can cut your airline bill by 10 to 50 percent or more.

Travel during "Low Season." If you can avoid travel from May through September, you'll find prices much lower, with (except at Christmas) the best deals between mid-November and mid-March. That's often not possible, of course, but if your family can go during a winter school holiday, your airfare may be less than half the summer rate. Of course there are drawbacks. Weather is less pleasant and attractions are often open shorter hours, but a winter trip might be possible even when a summer trip would break the family budget.

Avoid flying on weekends. Prices often are 5 to 10 percent higher on Friday, Saturday, and Sunday. Fly midweek and save. Stay in

solid international ex-perience, who books a lot of international travel and has traveled widely herself, her ideas and recommendations can be invaluable to you. An agent who specializes in cruises or group tours, on the other hand, won't provide nearly the same range of services—he doesn't know much more about the subject than *you* do! It's a mistake to just walk into a travel agency and ask to book a ticket to Paris; talk to several agents and pick the most knowledgeable, the one who seems most genuinely interested in helping your family with its adventure.

A travel agent who knows you're looking for inexpensive tickets to a particular destination can keep an eye open for sales that can save you hundreds of dollars per ticket, can help you sort through airlines and consolidators that are less

Paris at least a week. *The best rates are frequently offered for stays of between 7 and 30 days. Business travelers like short stays, and airlines squeeze as much as they can from corporate travelers.*

Check prices at all nearby airports. Prices can vary by 10 to 20 percent and more between airports just an hour's drive apart. If you're lucky enough to have several airports to choose among, you'll almost certainly find different prices at some of them. The closest might be the cheapest—or it might not be.

Be willing to make connections. If you want to travel nonstop, airlines might charge you a higher price for the convenience. True story: Some passengers who live in Cincinnati, Ohio, drive 50 miles to Dayton, Ohio, (the Lains' home base) and fly from the Dayton airport to Cincinnati to connect with a flight leaving for their destination. It's sometimes much cheaper to do that than for them to simply drive to the nearby Cincinnati airport and fly nonstop. Of course that makes no sense. But big companies don't have to make sense.

Check out consolidators. These are companies that buy blocks of tickets from airlines and resell them at prices lower than the airlines charge individual customers. They frequently advertise in the travel sections of large Sunday newspapers. A travel agent can help steer you toward more reputable consolidators. Investigate foreign carriers. Sometimes

than reliable, and can monitor ticket prices even *after* you've bought your seats, to help you qualify for a refund if an airline offers special sale prices later. Very few people who use the Web continue to check prices after they have their seats.

Many travel agencies that charge fees will waive them for regular customers or customers who spend a certain minimum amount (and airline tickets for a whole family will probably qualify).

There are advantages to using the Web as a tool, too:

• You can check prices for yourself, and read the restrictions and conditions. This can be time-consuming over a

you can get a good price on a flight that just stops in Paris on its way to another country. Sometimes, too, flights that involve an overnight stay in the home country of a foreign airline are deeply discounted.

Look for frequent flier deals. Some airlines offer big mileage bonuses to new members. Taking a whole family on a trip might yield enough miles to qualify for a free ticket or two for your next trip.

Watch for sales. Airlines have sales just like any other business. If you'd bought tickets at a higher price, they will normally credit you with the difference, less a service fee. Here, too, a travel agent can keep an eye open for you, because the agent checks prices every day, something you probably won't do after you've bought your tickets.

Follow those guidelines and you can flop down in your airplane seat comfortable that, even if you haven't paid the absolute lowest price on the plane, you've come as close as someone can who has a life devoted to something other than monitoring websites eighteen hours a day.

modem, however, because to get the best price, you need to check several airports, airlines, and connections, something that's time-consuming for the inexperienced.

• Some websites allow you to type in your destination and will automatically e-mail you if prices on that route drop more than a specified percentage. Again, you'll need to monitor multiple itineraries to get the best price.

• Some websites allow you to name your own price, enter how much you're willing to pay for a ticket, and they notify you if any itinerary matches that price. This is a great idea, but the tradeoff is that you have complete lack of control over airline and connection city (usually one or two connections are required). Sometimes, too, you're required to enter a credit card number and you'll be billed automatically for the tickets if your desired price is found—no chance to reconsider if the airline is one with a poor safety record, or if you're routed from Pittsburgh to Paris—via San Francisco!

Perhaps the best approach is to use a combination of strategies. I now check out prices and routings myself on the Web, so I know what my options are and how prices are running. Then I talk to my travel agent and *she* keeps track for me. Sometimes I end up with a flight I found myself on the Web. But more often she's able to beat my price eventually, usually by a substantial margin. Finding good airfares is what she does for a living; I'm just an amateur, and don't want to devote ten or fifteen hours a week to searching for a bargain fare—I have other things to do. This combination approach has saved us a substantial amount of money over the years.

The chapter World Wide Web Information on page 267 will give you some of the best airline-booking websites available.

Tip: Even after you've got your lowest fare, ask about gateway airports. One airline I often fly goes to Paris through two different U.S. cities. From one airport the plane is always packed. The other is seldom more than half full. On one recent trip, weather problems caused me to be rerouted and I flew to Paris jammed into a plane with no empty seats. Coming home I was on my originally-scheduled flight, one of just 40 passengers on a plane seating more than 200. I had an entire row to myself and plenty of room to stretch out for a nap. It was like flying First Class with bad food!

Packing

If you're driving to Paris in a big car, packing is not much of an issue for you. Take as much as you want. Take *two* of everything. Take *two cars!* It doesn't matter. If you're flying or taking the train, however, you're limited to what you can carry—and in the case of an airplane, how much the airline will *let* you bring.

We've all seen people schlepping through airports dragging most of the contents of their houses with them. I always wonder how long they expect to be gone! We've spent as long as five weeks abroad with only one checked bag and one carry-on. It's possible to manage on even less. It's easy. Just follow this rule: *Take only half of what you think you'll need.* That's all there is to it. Decide what you need for the trip and take only half of it. It really works.

Another approach. Pack whatever you can carry (no fair using the wheels on your suitcase) for a half mile (or 1 kilometer). You're allowed to set it down only once. If you can carry your luggage that far, you've packed well.

There's no point in hauling a piece of clothing halfway around the world to wear one time. The people you encounter haven't seen your wardrobe before and won't remember you after you're

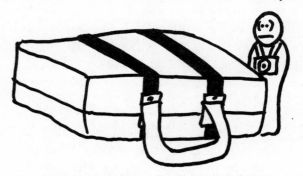

Pack wisely and this won't be you!

gone, so if they see you wearing the same outfit twice, your humiliation will be minimized. Unless the weather is hot, it's really OK to wear the same shirt more than once between washings.

And I'll promise this: If you leave something essential behind, you can buy it in France; stores in Paris are pretty well stocked.

Each member of the family should take a carry-on bag with a change of clothes (in the unlikely event that your checked bags take a detour) and the things they will want for the layover and flight. But it's silly to check even one suitcase per person for a trip of less than two weeks, even though the airlines permit two checked bags per passenger. No one needs to be burdened with that much stuff! One checked suitcase for every two people is perfect for a trip like this. They can take turns carrying it.

Do keep an eye on what your kids pack, even the older ones. They shouldn't turn up in Paris with nothing but old jeans and tee-shirts, or with only flouncy, frilly dresses. Help them balance the practical with the favorite, the appropriate with the casual.

In the summer, expect temperatures in Paris to be in the low to mid 80s Fahrenheit (28 Celsius) during the day and near 60°F (15°C) at night. Winter temperatures will typically run near 45°F in the daytime and 30°F at night (from 8°C to -1°C). If you wear layers, putting more on for colder weather, taking them off for warmer, you'll have more flexibility than if you take very heavy clothing in the winter. Stick to one basic color and its complement so anything can be worn with anything else. Here's how to pack for a trip of one to three weeks:

Packing Your Suitcase

This is where you put things you don't need on the flight and could live without if your baggage is diverted to Oslo. *Never* put money, passports, tickets, or film in checked luggage. Here's the list:

- 1-2 pairs of trousers or skirts
- shorts for warm-weather active pursuits
- 1 or (if really necessary) 2 pairs of shoes
- 3-5 shirts or blouses
- 6-8 sets of underwear
- sweater
- 6-10 pairs of socks or hose
- sleepwear
- toiletries
- umbrella

Remember that you can wash out small items like socks and underwear in the sink. If you're staying for much more than a week, take an evening to do a load or two of laundry instead of carrying enough clothes for the entire trip.

Don't forget that you have more clothes than are listed above: Unless your flight is booked on All Bare Air, you've got the clothes you're traveling in. It's surprising how often people don't remember to count those. Unless you're going to some very fancy places—with kids? yeah, right—a suit is unnecessary. But be sure that some of your clothes are what Europeans refer to as "smart casual": shirts with collars but no words, trousers other than denim, and shoes that aren't made for sports. Everyone can wear neat, comfortable clothes for general sightseeing but restaurants above the fast-food category frown on tee-shirts, jeans, and sneakers. Remind your kids: You're a guest in somebody else's country; just as you adapt to your host's preferences when you visit someone's house, you extend the same courtesy when you visit another country.

Packing Your Carry-on

Airlines are cracking down on excessive and oversized carry-on bags but they're not always sure themselves what that means.

When I checked in for a recent trip to Paris, two ticket agents and a supervisor fought angrily over the rules that applied to my bags—lots more entertaining than the in-flight movie!

Use your carry-on for important or expensive items like medicine or cameras, for things you want during the flight, and for a change of clothes in case your suitcase does take that Oslo sidetrip. Each person should carry a hearty snack like a couple of granola bars or bag of trail mix. It's becoming more common for airlines to have passengers board the plane, then make everyone sit there while they wait for a storm front to move past, for a lavatory to be repaired, or for the flight crew to finish its card game. If dinner is delayed for three hours (as we've had happen), it's nice to have iron rations to stem the hunger pangs.

Here's the list of what to pack in your carry-on:
- a change of clothes
- maps and guidebook (*Paris for Families* would be a good choice)
- camera and film
- any electrical equipment (radio, travel alarm, etc.)
- your snack
- in-flight entertainment (books, magazines, games, etc.)
- your journal or notebook
- medical supplies and prescriptions: *never* put these in checked bags!
- gum or hard candies for takeoff and landing

It's also a good idea to take a bottle of water. Long flights are dehydrating, and the beverage carts don't come around when you're really parched.

Leave your electric grooming supplies at home, if you can, especially if you're coming from somewhere, like North America, that uses a different voltage standard than France's 220v power. Your hair drier and electric razor won't work here unless you also bring a power converter (which doesn't always work well) and special plug adaptor. Even if your appliance is dual voltage or 220, you'll still probably need an adaptor to make the plug fit Parisian wall sockets, which require plugs with round pins. It's easier to let your hair air dry and to shave with a blade. (And I'd tell you the same thing even if I *weren't* a guy with thinning hair and a beard!)

Packing Yourself

Never put your passport or your money in any travel bag; keep them with you. You can't afford to get separated from these. But if you're traveling with a lot of money or traveler's checks, *please* don't carry all your money in your wallet or purse! Spend a little for a nylon money belt to wear under your trousers or skirt, or a neck pouch to wear under your shirt. Most of your money should be there, with only a 1-day supply of cash in your wallet. Both Mom and Dad should have one, and split the family treasury between them. Violent crime is rare in Europe, but bag-snatching and pick-pocketing is not.

What Else to Take

We have a large nylon bag that squashes down to almost nothing. We toss it in the bottom of a suitcase for the trip over and if we've bought more gifts and souvenirs than expected, we pack our dirty clothes in the nylon bag for the trip home and put our goodies in sturdier bags. We can also use it while we're abroad as a bag for dirty clothes and to haul things to the local launderette.

An inflatable pillow makes a good addition. I pack one in my carry-on because it feels good behind my back on a long flight, and sometimes is handy in a hotel or apartment where the pillows are just not quite thick enough for comfort.

A Word about Cameras and Film

Never put your film in checked luggage. Airlines use high-intensity scanners that *will* ruin it. Carry your film in your carry-on and ask that it be hand inspected. Most (but not all) airports will do that on request. To be on the safe side, consider buying a lead-lined film bag. The investment is worth it for photographs that can't be replaced. When security officials see this impenetrable black bag on the scanner, they'll give you a hand inspection anyway. Get a heavy-duty bag if you have film faster than ISO 400, because the higher the film speed, the more sensitive it is to x-rays.

Note that airport officials everywhere will tell you their scanners won't harm your film. *That is not true and they know it!* All three of the world's major film manufacturers—Kodak, Fuji, and Agfa—strongly recommend that film be hand inspected, not scanned. Why don't airports tell the truth? Because it's faster and more convenient for them not to have to hand inspect things. One or two passes through the x-ray for a slow film probably won't make much of a difference in amateur prints, but the effect is cumulative, is more pronounced on faster film, and is deadly for professionals.

Let the kids take cameras, too. You can get them each their own inexpensive one, or a camera they can share. The photos they take will be different from the ones their parents shoot, and often of things Mom and Dad don't notice. You can get handy disposable cameras almost everywhere, but if you're bringing them home before having the film processed, you must protect them the same way you protect your film, and that's bulky. An inexpensive point-and-shoot camera is a much better choice.

Keeping a Travel Journal

Give each of the kids a notebook and pen before you leave, and get one for yourself. Everybody thinks about photos on a trip, but just as meaningful is a journal that will help you remember what you did, when you did it, and what you felt about it. Encourage (but don't force) everyone to spend fifteen minutes a day writing about what they saw, did, and thought. They might write about topics like the best and worst things that happened that day, the neatest and strangest things they saw, what they bought, even what the weather was like and what they had at mealtimes. These things will help everyone remember the trip more vividly in years to come. Remember that these are personal diaries, though. The authors don't have to share their thoughts with anybody. The discipline of keeping a journal is still sometimes hard for me, but I wouldn't part with mine any more than I would with my photos.

A Trip Notebook

It's also handy for someone to keep a notebook filled with essential information. Many people (including the author) always record all their flight information, traveler's checks numbers, passport numbers, phone numbers to report lost credit cards, addresses of people to send postcards to, emergency phone numbers back home, their budget, essential and useful information about the place they're visiting (from the telephone number of the police to the frequencies of favorite radio stations). We also keep track of our spending there, recording purchases, noting traveler's checks cashed and bank machine withdrawals made. It's nice to have all that in one place, and it's helpful to be able to see exactly how much we spent on a previous trip as we make plans for a return. We've also had U.S. customs officials agree just to look at our list of purchases rather than rooting through our bags. We must have honest faces.

Enjoying the Tedium

The worst thing about travel is that it can be so *boring*. You sit down in a car or a train. You ride. And ride. And ride some more. Or worse, you sit around in airports. You sit around in airplanes. You stand in long lines. If you have an 8-hour international flight, your day will be a lot longer than that. You might spend a half-hour driving to your local airport, an hour waiting for your flight to leave, 1½ hours flying to your connecting city where you'll face a 3-hour layover. Then you'll spend 8 hours in the air, an hour clearing immigration and customs, and another hour getting from the airport to your apartment or hotel. That's a 16-hour day before you can even *think* about sightseeing! That's mighty hard on kids (and on their parents, too!).

If you're making a trip like this with a family, you need to make sure that the younger kids, especially, know what to expect, and you need to plan activities to keep them from getting bored and whiney. Teens are pretty self-sufficient, but to younger children there doesn't seem to be much difference between a 4-hour layover and one that lasts the rest of their lives!

Whether you're going to Paris by car, train, plane, bicycle, or on horseback, each person should have his or her own carry-on bag. Besides the items listed earlier in the packing section, make sure the kids have

- a snack
- two or three books
- another snack
- a tape player or handheld video game
- more food
- a deck of cards
- something else to eat
- a book of puzzles and a pencil

You get the idea. Packing a variety of things to do is important because kids have short attention spans. One book won't last a

10-year-old sixteen hours! But how you pass the time depends on where you are.

Airport Layovers

Those two words—airport layovers—freeze the blood of most travelers, who believe that the only thing worse than being stuck in an airport for three hours would be to spend them in a dentist's chair. Possibly. But get this: We've actually *scheduled* long layovers for ourselves, arranged our flights so we've had five to eight hours between them.

If you are connecting through a city with good transportation from the airport to the center city, you can take a mini-vacation that will set a great tone for your family's big adventure. We've built layovers into connections like Philadelphia and Washington, D.C., which have fast, efficient subways into the city. Arrive, stash your bags in a locker, find the train, and go on a sightseeing binge. Many other cities offer the same advantage. London's Heathrow, for instance, has just added an express train into the city from the airport. Two vacations for the price of one!

If you don't have the time or transportation facilities to make this possible, you'll have to make the best of your airport captivity.

Try to make your layover as short as possible, of course—but without pushing it too close. Leaving too little time between flights puts you at the mercy of weather delays and mechanical problems: one glitch and your Paris flight leaves without you ... or at least without your luggage.

This is not making good use of a layover!

So just plan on *at least* a 90-minute layover. You can spend some of that time feeding the troops and making sure everybody's water bottle is full. Let everyone browse through the newsstand and pick out one more magazine to take along. Pack some change, because every airport now has a row of video games –and sometimes a whole arcade of games—somewhere nearby. Start a family chess tournament; a small board with magnetic pieces takes up very little room. There are compact travel versions of many popular board games.

People-watching games are fun in airports and busy railway stations. Before you leave home, make a list of things to look for, like tee-shirts with ten different university names, hats from three different football teams, a stroller or pram with twin babies, a person reading a Stephen King novel, a tearful farewell, a tearful reunion. Airports and train stations are interesting places with a lot to see and do if you come prepared and don't just say, "Sit down and be patient." You've spent months planning this trip. It's *hard* to be patient, especially for kids who have helped with the planning.

In Transit

Even a 3-hour layover is easier than the trip itself, however. Airports and train stations have a constant flow of people and lots of room to roam. Once the journey starts, though, the pace around you slows. On a train, at least, scenery can be diverting for awhile. On an airplane there isn't much scenery, especially if you're on an overnight flight.

Try to arrange window seats for the kids. Unless it's dark, they'll have the best view of whatever there is to see, and it will give them a wall to lean against if they want to go to sleep, something that's harder on an aisle with traffic constantly brushing past.

On an overnight flight, try to get kids to skip the in-flight movie and sleep. Leaving the headphones off for the first fifteen minutes will usually be enough. Play quiet games with the family member in the next seat. Suggest making the first entry in the travel journal, writing about the layover, what the inside of the plane or train is like, and how things are going so far.

Most airlines, with several days' advance notice, will prepare special meals for the kids, something like a hamburger and fries, that they will enjoy more than the regular menu choices of mystery meat over rice or gray fish in gray sauce.

Waiting is never easy, and it's even harder for excited kids, but if children are prepared for the trip—if they've helped plan it from the beginning and know what to expect in transit—they'll be better travelers. Make them feel like this is *their* trip, too, not just Mom and Dad's trip that they're coming along on. Use their ideas, plan activities that *they* like. Mom and Dad will have chances another time to plan trips around their own interests. But a *family* trip like this can be an exciting *family* event if everyone is involved. Even the drive, the train ride, the flight can be a chance to talk together, to play together, to be excited together about sharing a terrific experience together. Attitude is everything on a trip like this, and with such a payoff in sight— Paris!—travel is only tedious if you let it be.

Recommendations

✔ Make the travel as stress free as possible with leisurely layovers if you're flying, frequent stops if you're driving. Remember: This is supposed to be fun!

✔ If you can, see some sights along the way by using your layover or travel cities creatively.

✔ Don't overpack. No holiday is worth a hernia. If you forget something, buy it in Paris and call it a souvenir.

For the latest updates to Paris for Families, check our
page on the Web at:

www.interlinkbooks.com/parisforfamilies.html

4. Arrival!

This is it—the payoff! You've planned your trip for months, read everything you could get your hands on, talked about it until friends or co-workers have threatened to have your mouth sewn shut. And now—Now!— the vacation begins. All you have to do is to get to your apartment and the fun can start. But that's your first challenge, and it's a bit intimidating if you've never been to Paris before and are unsure of your language skills.

Relax! Paris is easy to find your way around.

Getting To Your Apartment

Arriving by Car

If you've driven from somewhere else in Europe, you will have already made arrangements about what to do with your car. The person with whom you booked your apartment or hotel has told you exactly how to get where you're going and where to park when you get there.

Parisians claim, with an odd pride, to have some of the most frenetic and furious traffic in the world. Paris streets *are* busy— no doubt about it. And there are certainly streets that no sane first-time visitor should try the first day—maybe ever; *Etoile*, the roundabout around the Arc de Triomphe, springs to mind. But honestly, the traffic in Paris is, on the whole, no worse than traffic in *any* big city. If you can drive in Chicago, Munich, or Manchester, you can drive in Paris.

Be sensible, though. Time your arrival for late morning or early afternoon if at all possible. Paris rush hour is no time to tackle unfamiliar roadways, and arriving after dark can make it impossible to see signs and difficult to navigate narrow, unfamiliar streets.

A large motorway called the *Périphérique* surrounds Paris, and the major highways empty onto it. ("A" highways are the most important routes.) Use the Périphérique to get as close as you can to your apartment. If you are coming from the east but staying near the Eiffel Tower, for example, you'll find it much faster to drive all the way around Paris on the Périphérique than to take a shorter route through the center of the city: It's shorter in distance only!

Both driver and navigator should study the map before you get to Paris, and mark your route with colored ink. Take time to learn unfamiliar road signs,

> ***Tip:*** *Major highways entering Paris from the north have low numbers and get larger as you go clockwise around the Périphérique. The A1 is straight north, the A3 comes in from the east, the A4 from the southeast, and so on.*

although most highway markings are becoming standard in the EU. Take your time and don't get stressed; this is a holiday. It's supposed to be fun! You *will* get where you're going!

Just a few reminders: First, make sure your automobile insurance is in order and will cover you in France. Second, get

Arrival!

an International Driver's License if you are from outside the European Union. Drivers in France must be at least 18 years old.

Arriving by Train

Paris has six major railway terminals. **Gare St-Lazare** and **Gare Montparnasse** serve mostly other destinations in France. The busiest international station is **Gare du Nord**, with arrivals from Britain (via the Channel Tunnel), Scandinavia, Germany, and the Low Countries. Nearby **Gare de l'Est** serves mostly Germany and Austria. Travelers from Spain and Portugal usually arrive at **Gare d'Austerlitz**, and those from Italy and Switzerland arrive at **Gare de Lyon**.

Wherever you arrive, you should have little trouble in getting to your apartment. The easiest way, of course, is to take a taxi, and you'll never have trouble finding one near a railway station. If you're unsure of making yourself understood in French, have the address of your apartment or hotel written down clearly, including the postcode, which tells the arrondissement, or city district. It's a good idea to have the location of your Paris home marked on your map, too, in case it's in a part of town your driver doesn't know well. That's seldom a problem. Chapter 6 will tell you all you need to know about Paris taxis.

If you're confident of your navigation skills and are not overburdened with luggage, you can make your first foray onto the Paris Metro or RER. Every rail station has two or more lines running through it and, probably with no more than one change of train, you can get quite close to your apartment or hotel. The Paris Metro was designed so nowhere in the city is more than 500 meters (550 yards) from a Metro station, so with a good sense of direction and a good map, you ought to be able to walk those last few hundred meters. Details on the Metro are also in Chapter 6.

Arriving by Air

Paris is served by two major airports. Roissy-Charles de Gaulle is north of the city and Orly is south. CDG is the larger of the two and handles more international traffic, but it doesn't matter where you arrive: Getting to central Paris is simple from both and the process is almost identical.

Take note of which terminal you arrive at and jot it down on your ticket envelope. It will make your life easier when you go home again. Each airport has two terminals: **CDG-1** and **CDG-2** at De Gaulle, and **Ouest** (west) and **Sud** (south) at Orly. When you go home, you'll leave from the same terminal you arrived at, unless you're flying a different airline for some reason. The main international terminals are CDG-1 and Orly Sud—but there are always exceptions.

If you hold a passport from a country in the European Union, things are simple: You leave the plane, go through the line for EU residents (much faster!), collect your bags, and get on with your life. If you're from the rest of the world it will take just a little longer. But don't be intimidated—it's not difficult. More tourists go to France than anywhere else in the world and very few of them are as smart as you! If they can manage, you can manage!

The Landing Card: If your flight originated outside of France and you're not a citizen of France or another country in the European Union, your process of arriving by air will actually begin an hour or so before you land. After breakfast (on overnight flights) or the last passage of the beverage cart, flight attendants will be around with landing cards for you to fill out. You'll be asked to write your name, nationality, flight number, and Paris address on the card. Keep these papers with your passports. If you have questions, ask the flight attendant on the plane; the immigration officers at the airport won't help you—they'll just send you to the end of the line again.

Arrival!

One of the easiest things in the world to do is to go through the correct procedure after an inter-national flight. That's because there's no other choice. When you get off the plane, grab your carry-on and just follow the crowd; it's impossible to go astray, take the wrong turn, or get lost. It's a lot like the cattle drives in old cowboy movies—all the cows are herded along the trail by the cowhands... no chance to get away. (Like most fathers, I am often an embarrassment to my children. I *always* have to struggle against the urge to say "Moooo!" as my fellow passengers and I are herded through the landing process. Immigration officials in every country I know take a dim view of this.) In any case, most important directional signs are in English as well as French. Other languages are less consistently represented.

Any Porte in the Storm

It's easy to make your way through either Paris airport. Signs are in French and English and often a smattering of other languages, and employees at information desks speak many languages. Finding trans-portation into central Paris seldom even involves talking to a human, though. It's just a matter of going to the right porte (door or gate). Most transportation leaves at intervals of every 15 to 20 minutes.

CHARLES DE GAULLE	Terminal 1	Terminal 2A & 2C	Terminal 2B & 2D
Taxis	Porte 16	Porte 7	Porte 7
Air France Bus (Etoile)	Porte 34	Porte 5	Porte 6
Air France Bus (Montp.)	Porte 26	Porte 2	Porte 1
Roissybus	Porte 30	Porte 10	Porte 12
RATP buses	Porte 30	Porte 10	Porte 12
RER shuttle	Porte 28	Porte 5	Porte 6

ORLY	Terminal Sud		Terminal Ouest
Taxis	Porte H		Hall 2
Air France Bus	Porte F5		Hall 3
Orlybus	Porte H4		Porte C
Orlyval/RER-B	Porte E, F		Hall 2
RER-C shuttle	Porte H1		Hall 3

Immigration and Customs: Your first stop will be at the Immigration checkpoint. The line is always long but it usually moves surprisingly fast. Have your passports and landing cards in hand when you get to the front of the line, and go to the checkpoint together. Hand your papers to the inspector, who will keep the landing cards, and look at your passports and your family to make sure you are who you claim to be. You might be asked a couple of questions about where you're staying or why you're visiting France. Just give direct answers and don't make jokes. The inspector doesn't want to make conversation and will not be amused by your humor. (It's widely believed that international law forbids countries to hire people with a sense of humor to be immigration officials.) Be pleasant, be polite, and you'll be on your way in no more than a minute.

Now it's time to retrieve your luggage. Again, follow the herd to the baggage carousels, or the signs that say *Bagages*. Remember your flight number: It will be posted at the carousel where your bags will emerge. Count on this: If you have two bags, yours will be the first and last ones off the plane. Baggage handlers, it's rumored, have to go to school for *years* to learn to separate luggage in the most inconvenient way.

Once you have your luggage, again it's time to follow the crowd. Everyone's going to customs. You probably can go through the Green channel (nothing to declare). The Red channel is for people bringing in items to sell, or Parisians returning from trips with more than their duty-free allowance. It's possible, but unlikely, that a Customs inspector will ask you to open one or more of your bags. If you're unlucky and asked to do so, comply cheerfully and the inspection will go quickly. Remind the kids *not* to make jokes about leaving their bomb or drugs in the other bag. In airports, those things are not considered jokes.

That's all there is to it. You leave the Customs area and enter the Arrival Hall. At last, after all the planning and excitement:

Arrival!

Welcome to Paris!

Getting to your apartment or hotel: One last step and you can take off your shoes and relax. You're almost home. You have three choices for getting into central Paris from each airport—taxi, bus, and train. Each has advantages and disadvantages. The sidebar *Any Porte in the Storm* will tell you exactly where to find each at your airport.

By Taxi (both airports): The chief advantage here is door-to-door convenience; the chief disadvantages are cost and room. Many taxis will not take more than three people, and when they do, they charge extra. They may also charge extra for excess luggage. If there are four people in your family, taxis are difficult. Five or more? Forget it! A taxi from Orly probably will cost 150F to 250F, perhaps more, depending on where you're going. From CDG the fare will be at least 250F, probably more. No, a taxi might occasionally be a good choice for a family, but not often.

By Bus (CDG): This is the easiest—and slowest—approach if you're staying close to one of the drop-off points. Both the RATP (public transport agency) and Air France run buses to various parts of the city. If you're staying west, there's Air France bus to *Porte Maillot* and *Etoile*, and if you are staying south or southwest, there's an Air France bus to *Montparnasse*. For central apartments, the Roissybus from RATP to *Opéra* is the best choice. RATP bus No. 350 goes to *Gare de l'Est* on the north and No. 351 goes to *Place de la Nation* on the east. Fares are less than 50F per person and the trip will take from 45 minutes to well over an hour, depending on traffic. You should have no trouble getting a taxi or changing to the Metro at any drop-off point.

By Bus (Orly): The process from Orly is the same but with fewer choices. Air France buses go to *Invalides* and *Montparnasse*, and RATP's Orlybus runs to *Denfert-Rochereau* on the city's southeast side. Cost is about 40F and the trip takes about an hour. There are no convenient buses from Orly to the center, north, or east; you'll have to transfer to the Metro or another bus, or get a taxi, if that's where you want to go.

By RER (CDG): The suburban rail network, called the RER, is usually the best overall choice. A free shuttle bus will take you to the train station for Line B, where again, it's just a matter of following the crowd. A ticket into central Paris costs about 50F and the trip takes 35 to 45 minutes, depending on how far you're going. (Children under 11 are half-price.) Major stops are *Gare du Nord* (north), *Châtelet-Les Halles* (central), and *Denfert-Rochereau* (south). At any of these you can transfer for free to the Metro or grab a taxi.

By RER (Orly): You have two choices of RER trains from Orly. RER-B is the same central Paris line that runs to CDG. You reach it via the *Orlyval* monorail from the airport to the Antony RER station. Fare is about 60F total (children half-price) for Orlyval and the RER. Travel time is 8 minutes on the monorail and about 40 minutes on the train. If you're staying on the Left Bank, your best choice might be RER-C, which goes to *Gare d'Austerlitz, St-Michel*, and *Invalides*. A shuttle bus will take you from the airport to the RER station at Rungis. Travel time is about 45 minutes on the train. Fare is about 50F, with a slight discount for children. Transfers to the Metro are easy in central Paris, and taxis are plentiful.

Taking the RER is simple. Don't be intimidated if your command of French is limited—or nonexistent! Yes, nearly all signs on the train are in French, but if you look at the map and know where you're going, and pay attention to the names of one or two stops before your destination, you'll be just fine. It's virtually impossible to board the wrong train. From the stations, just follow the signs that say *Direction Paris*. There's

Tip: When you buy your ticket, ask for a free, pocket-sized map of the Paris Metro, RER, and bus system called a Petit Plan de Paris. *Every member of your family should carry one.*

a clear map of the route in each train car. If you've been on an all-night flight you may feel a bit befogged, but remember that millions of people have managed this quite nicely and none of them have ever failed to get where they were going. Relax and enjoy.

Home at Last

Most people *hate* traveling... even travel writers! It's *being* someplace that's fun. There's no feeling quite like finally getting to the place you're going, walking through the door, collapsing onto the first piece of soft furniture you see, and letting out a sigh of relief that sounds like a hole in the Goodyear Blimp. We made it! And the longer the trip... the more planning involved... and the longer you've been looking forward to it— then the deeper and more satisfying the sigh.

Then there's a brief feeling of panic. *Now what?* That's normal, too. A trip like this takes a lot of time to plan, costs a lot of money, and is the absolute focus of everybody's vacation. You don't want anybody to be disappointed, but ever since you got up this morning, your whole attention has been on the *act* of traveling. Now you're under pressure to have fun! So where do you start?

Take it slow. Whether you've just arrived after a cramped 12-hour flight from Los Angeles or a comfortable 3-hour train ride from London, everybody's feeling a bit (maybe more than a bit!) frazzled and road-weary just now. It's a mistake to just dump your bags in the middle of the room and dash out to see the Eiffel Tower. It's been there for well over a century; it will still be there in a couple of hours, after everyone has had a little time to unwind. This is especially important traveling with kids. Remember the first axiom of family travel: *Most of the time, the mood of the group will be determined by its most tired member.*

How much you can do today depends on three things:

❶ How you got here

❷ How far you've traveled

❸ What time you arrive

If you've had a flight of more than two or three hours, be careful of doing too much walking today. Your feet swell in the pressurized cabin and doing too much walking too soon will raise blisters that will make the next week absolutely miserable. On the other hand, if you arrived by train or car, you need to stretch your legs, and a long walk will feel good and restore circulation to legs that have been inactive for too long.

If you've come a very long way—on an overnight flight from North America, for example—you are at the greatest risk from jetlag. No matter how excited your mind is to finally be here, your body couldn't care less. Smaller kids aren't aware of what their bodies are telling them; they only listen to their minds, and parents will have to help them cope in some other way than by being crabby. There's a solution below.

When you arrive makes difference, too. Flights from North America usually arrive early in the morning, so those travelers may be in their apartments well before noon, but with bodies that have been up all night. Other flights and trains may turn up at almost any time, so their passengers might have most of the day ahead of them, or very little. Drivers can, of course, pretty much arrive when they want, but from a traffic perspective, midday is—let's not say *best*. Let's say *least bad*.

Getting Organized

Let's look at your first six steps after you arrive at your apartment or hotel:

Step 1: Your first task is to **Unpack**. It's an ironclad guarantee that no matter how much you'd rather save putting things away until later, you'll feel a lot less like doing it then than you do now.

Step 2: This applies only to travelers who have arrived on overnight flights. It's *essential* for your kids... and for you as well. Everybody else can skip this step. **Go to sleep.** Right. Take a nap. That seems foolish as you sit in your chair at home planning the trip. Why spend goodness-knows-how-much money on the trip of a lifetime, and then spend the first two hours sleeping? But unless everybody slept four or five hours on the plane, *don't* skip this step. You've had a very long and exhausting day so far, and while it may be noon in Paris, your body thinks it's still 6 AM. (if you've come from New York or Montréal, for example) and that you've been up all night. If you trust this advice and take a 2- or 3-hour nap *now*, you will have no jetlag problems. If you ignore this advice, you'll have to drag yourself through the next three days. Don't oversleep, though, because if you do, you won't sleep well tonight. Set an alarm. Tonight, go to bed at your regular time or a bit earlier and tomorrow your body clock will be set on Paris time and you'll be ready for anything.

Step 3: Now take your first look at Paris: **Explore your neighborhood.** This is where you'll be spending the next week or two, so you want to begin to feel at home here as soon as you can. If you're staying in an apartment, you'll want to look for local food stores, bakeries, and markets. Unless your apartment has laundry facilities available you'll want to find a self-service laundry. Go several blocks in each direction so you know where the nearest Metro stations and bus stops are located and note on your *Petit Plan* which lines they're on and where they go. On your neighborhood walk you can also find the nearest post office, cash machine or bank, a kiosk or tobacconist where you can buy newspapers and magazines, somewhere to buy some snacks, and a few tempting places to eat. The reason for renting an apartment is to Live Like a Local, shopping where Parisians shop, living your lives, in many ways, as they live theirs. Your family will have a much greater sense of place that way than visitors who stay in hotels. Even if you do stay in a hotel, though, you'll want to look for many of the same things on your neighborhood walk.

Step 4: **Have a meal**. You've had a busy day already, and probably a long one. Now's the time to refortify yourself. On your neighborhood walk you've probably seen several restaurants or cafés you thought you'd like to try. Go ahead. Check out the menus of several—menus are always displayed out front—and go in the most interesting for lunch or dinner. Everyone is sure to be famished by now, with all the travel and excitement. If you have little or no French, this might be the moment you've been worried about: "Can I communicate?" Sure you can. The next chapter will make things a little easier for you, and I've never heard of a tourist starving to death in Paris. Remember, these places are in the business of selling food. They *want* you to come in. After the meal, everyone will feel full of good food and of a renewed excitement for the trip.

Step 5: After everyone is fed, **Do basic shopping**. You need food for the apartment, perhaps some other supplies. The kids will enjoy wandering through the grocery store looking at familiar brands with unfamiliar labels, at products they can't decipher the use for, at the tremendous novelty of what they see. This might be a more exciting thing for some of them than their first glimpse of the Eiffel Tower, because it's so unexpected and, frankly, foreign. This is also a good time to stop at the nearest Metro station and buy your *Carte Orange* or a carnet or two of tickets so you're mobile. You'll learn all about this in Chapter 6.

Step 6: After the groceries are put away, and depending on what time it is, you might want to **Do some sightseeing**. Depending on when you arrived, by now it might be late and time for some of the kids to go to bed. Or it might be only 3 p.m. So decide where you want to go, look on your Metro map for the best route, and hop on a train. This is a great time to try it out. Before long everyone will be gazing wide-eyed up the Eiffel Tower, or strolling along the Seine across from Notre Dame, or jostling through the crowds on the Champs Élysées with the Arc de Triomphe looming ahead, saying "Wow! We did it! We're really in Paris!" Right then—that moment—will be one of the best moments your family has ever had together.

Recommendations

✔ Don't try to do *everything* on your first day in Paris. Get organized and the rest of the vacation will go more smoothly.

✔ If you had an overnight flight, take a nap, even if you don't think you need it. You do.

✔ You'll be walking more than usual, so be careful of blisters. Take it easy the first day.

Get your bearings from the neighborhood maps at Metro entrances

For the latest updates to *Paris for Families*, check our page on the Web at:

www.interlinkbooks.com/parisforfamilies.html

5. Food, French Style

S omewhere along the way you've heard that the French pay
serious attention to food... that its cuisine is a national
obsession... that dining is considered an important event,
not merely an opportunity for refueling... that gastronomical
nirvana is more avidly sought than the company of one's friends,
the stabilization of one's marriage, or the salvation of one's soul.

It's not that way at all.

It's more intense than that.

OK, OK, that's an exaggeration. But food *is* important in
France. Parisians eat out a lot and there's a ritual to mealtime
that baffles much of the rest of the world. First-time visitors to
Paris often—perhaps usually—feel like intruders in restaurants,
insecure and uncertain, afraid of making a blunder that will
incite the frown of a waiter or provoke outright scorn from the
maitre d'hôtel.

Relax. Parisians cultivate that image, but there's no reason at
all to be intimidated. With kids in tow, Mom and Dad are
probably not going to be dining at Maxim's on this trip anyhow.

Let's de-mystify the sacrament of dining in Paris by letting you know what to expect when you shop, and a bit about what will happen when you dine out. Despite the mystique, there's not that much to learn. But before we begin, there's one point you should keep in mind:

Despite the sophistication ascribed to them, Parisians are just ordinary people.

When you're at home, do you dine in elegant restaurants every night? Certainly not. Sometimes don't you just have macaroni and cheese in front of the television? Count on this: All over Paris tonight, people are eating macaroni and cheese in front of the television. It just sounds classier to call it *nouilles et fromage*.

Eating In

It's certainly a positive joy to eat out in Paris. The selection is wonderful and the food is delicious. But if you're staying in an apartment, you will probably want to take advantage of the ability to save a little money by doing at least some of your own cooking. In fact, you can save a *lot* of money that way. Fancy preparations aren't necessary; you can get those in restaurants. Simple, quick meals, the same recipes you prepare at home (even macaroni and cheese), are all you need. No one wants to spend too much of a vacation cooking, but relaxing over familiar food in your apartment after a busy day of sightseeing is a good way to unwind, and is especially comforting to the kids.

Grocery Stores

Wherever your apartment is in Paris, you're within a five-minute walk of a small grocery store. After all, Parisians have to eat, too, and even people who have cars (many people do not) are no more eager to battle the Paris traffic than you are. You won't find huge supermarkets like Sainsbury's or Safeway, at least not in the heart of Paris, but there are plenty of small and medium-sized stores like Franprix, which has locations all over the city. On your shopping excursion your first afternoon in Paris, you'll enjoy browsing through the store, and the kids will have a ball looking at unknown brands and enigmatic packaging. If you don't speak French, take along a small dictionary or that package of butter you thought you bought might turn out to be cream cheese!

Prices might be lower than you expect, no more than you're used to paying at home, and the selection will be as broad—perhaps more so. Just visit the cheese section, for example. The array is dizzying. An exasperated Charles De Gaulle is supposed to have once said in frustration, "How is anyone supposed to govern a people that makes 400 different kinds of cheese!"

If you'd like a little wine with your cheese, you can get a bottle for as little as 10F. (I didn't specify *good* wine, mind you. But it's quite drinkable.)

When you check out, you'll usually be expected to bag your purchases yourself. A rack of plastic bags will be just past the cash register. Stores will usually be open until 8 PM and often later, but may not be open at all on Sundays.

Don't buy everything at the grocery store, though. If you want to Live Like a Local, you'll want to make at least two more stops. They are very much worth it, both in terms of price and quality.

Produce Markets

Every neighborhood has a fruit and vegetable market nearby—often several. Prices here will be better even than at an inexpensive chain like Monoprix, and the selection and quality will be noticeably better. Almost everything is sold by weight. Little or nothing will be prepackaged.

One great thing about the produce markets is that they're apt to turn up just when you need them most as you wander around the city, and are ideal for getting everyone an inexpensive, nutritious snack. The most wonderful orange I ever ate was on a February day when I was weary of walking, famished, and as parched as an August afternoon. Just before I passed out (I was sure), I came upon a produce market a few blocks from Invalides, where I bought for 3F an orange that was bigger than most grapefruit of my acquaintance.

It was as sweet as honey. I ate it sitting in the Champ de Mars gazing up at the Eiffel Tower and soon, with my spirits lifted, my stomach full, my thirst abated, and my fingers sticky with orange juice, I set off renewed and refreshed.

The Bakery

It's possible to buy bread at the grocery store. But it's also possible to look at comic books in the Louvre. The question is, why would you want to? That's crazy! If you want to Live Like a Local, do what the French do—buy your bread fresh from the bakery next door or across the street.

Bakeries are everywhere, and it's almost impossible to find a bad one. Standards are high, because the French have bread with every meal and insist on having things done right. Indeed, the French eat 3.4 billion kilograms (7.4 billion pounds) a year! The sidebar *Flour Power* will tell you a bit more about this staple of the French table.

Unlike grocery-store bread, what you get from the bakery isn't loaded with preservatives; you'll want to get a fresh loaf every day. But bread comes in a large assortment of shapes and sizes, so there's never any need for waste. About all a day-old baguette is good for is pounding nails.

You can find all sorts of other specialty food stores for meat, fish, cheese—you hardly have to go to a general grocery store at all. But doing *all* your shopping at specialty stores can be time consuming when you're on holiday. Try these two, however. You'll feel very Parisian.

Eating Out

Yes, there are restaurants in Paris where you will be greeted at the door by a man in a tuxedo, shown to a table set with the finest china and crystal, and served a meal personally prepared by a chef with a whole galaxy of Michelin stars, all while a string quartet plays discreetly in the background. But probably not with a family.

There are several levels of eating out, and we'll talk here about the ones that are most useful for a family. The string quartet will have to wait, perhaps, for another book.

Food on the Go

Sometimes you don't want a meal; just a quick snack is plenty to keep complaints at bay. Well, remember to make sure everyone packs a filling snack like a few granola bars in their daypacks. Emergency rations like that can forestall a lot of grumbling and whining... and that's just from the parents! In the warm weather you'll have no trouble finding ice cream vendors, and a cold chocolate cone on a hot day is the best antidote in the world for afternoon hunger and fatigue. And we've already mentioned the neighborhood produce markets.

You won't have to look hard to find something a bit more substantial. In almost every park and near almost every important building, you'll find a stand selling a variety of refreshment. If you're just thirsty, you can get soft drinks, coffee, and bottled water. If you're hungry, you'll often find hot dogs available. (That was a surprise to this American, who thought hot dogs would be beneath the French palate. On the other hand, maybe mine is the palate they had in mind.) A better choice is a sandwich on half a baguette. You'll find a variety of fillings but ham or cheese are the most common. You might also see chicken or vegetarian sandwiches, the latter something of a portable salad.

The sandwiches aren't the overstuffed deli sort you might get on the street in someplace like New York, but they're filling and the bread is, as always, delicious. You'll find them everywhere— street-corner stands, parks, museum snack bars.

Better still are the crêpes! You'll see crêperies everywhere. Sometimes they're stores along the street and offer a wide variety of fillings, but often they're just part of the fast-food stands along the street. The kids will be fascinated watching them made, the thin batter poured out and continually smoothed to a delicate lightness with a little wooden mallet. You can usually choose *jambon* (ham), *fromage* (cheese), *mixte* (ham *and* cheese), and *chocolat* (which needs no translation). Crêpes are a delicious, inexpensive, and very French lunch or snack.

The ubiquitous international fast-food chains are well represented in Paris, and you can visit one if kids insist. We've found them most useful for cold drinks and convenient toilets, though. At least the Belgian hamburger restaurant Quick (you can't miss its bright red stores) provides a little variety from the inevitable American versions. And you'll notice one other quirk you might not expect. In Paris, even a pizza is served with a knife and fork.

The French use a knife & fork for almost everything

Cafés, Brasseries, Bistros, and Restaurants

Now we come to the sort of dining everyone associates with Paris, and that is, perhaps, most intimidating to visitors, especially those unsure of their language skills (or, perhaps, certain of their

complete *in*ability to speak
French!). But relax.
Parisian restaurants are
designed to create a
comfortable, secure atmosphere as well as to
showcase the chef's skills.
You're going to enjoy this
part of the trip.

Tip: Not everyone pays the same
price in a café. Customers
who choose outdoor seating
pay the highest price, and those sitting
inside are charged less. On a beautiful
sunny day in Paris, it's worth an extra few
francs to sit outdoors and become part of
the Parisian landscape.

There is a tremendous range of restaurants in Paris, even
within the categories above. Generally speaking, types of
restaurants can be categorized like this:

Cafés: These are the backbone of Paris eating. They are usually
open early, offering coffee and croissants for breakfast, simple
sandwiches, soups, and salads for lunch, and a light menu in the
evening, closing by 8 or 9 PM except in tourist areas. Cafés are
generally inexpensive, with lunch falling in the 40F to 70F
range. They are at their best when you're tired and footsore, and
you sit at an outdoor table to refresh yourself with a cup of
coffee or hot chocolate, a cold soft drink, or a glass of wine.

Brasseries: These are often noisy, crowded places with emphasis
on hearty foods like sausage and sauerkraut. Service is faster
than at some other places, and the menus are the most extensive
of any sort of Parisian eatery. Brasseries are usually open until
midnight or later. Expect to pay 50F to 150F for your meal.

Bistros: A bistro is often just a small restaurant, sometimes with
no more than 30 or 40 seats, with a relatively short menu, often
family-run, almost always featuring carefully prepared traditional
cooking. Prices for a meal can range from 75F to 200F or more.
Bistros always seem like the most "Parisian" place to eat. It's a
good idea to book a table a day or two ahead in a small bistro.

Some are open only for dinner, some at both lunch and dinner. You might find yourself sharing a long table with another group in the homey atmosphere.

Restaurants: Restaurants come in all configurations. At a restaurant you can expect an appetizer, main course, and dessert, and perhaps other courses as well. Restaurants are frequently open only at dinnertime and prices vary from 70F to "how-much-do-you-have?" Relatively few restaurants have dress codes; clean, neat clothing is all that's expected.

French law requires that all types of restaurants display their menus in the window, so you can easily see what kind of food is served and the price range before you go in. Well-behaved children are welcome in all restaurants, but don't expect to see a separate menu for children; they're not common. Because the pace is slow in Parisian restaurants, very young children will probably be happier in a café where service is faster and where sandwiches predominate.

An Evening at a Restaurant

In bistros and restaurants, you'll probably find that service is slower—much slower—than you're used to. The French believe a meal should be savored, lingered over, coaxed and caressed into yielding its most subtle flavors. Courses come slowly, leaving time for digestion and conversation. You won't even get coffee with your dessert: the waiter will bring it after you've finished. Even then, the bill will never just be brought to you—you'll have to ask for it.

This is simply the way it's done, and if you or the kids are not in the mood for a two-hour meal (at least!), stick to cafés and brasseries.

But by all means, try a restaurant at least once. Make an evening of it—that's the way Parisians prefer it, and you're temporary Parisians, after all. If you look at menus as you pass by, you'll find some astonishing bargains, set three-course dinners for as little as 65F! The tradeoff is that you're given only a choice of three or four items for each course, but what does that matter? The food will be exactly the same as if you'd ordered it à la carte. Bread is always included and is perfect for soaking up the tasty sauces.

Check the menu outside (using a dictionary, if necessary) to make selections before you go in, and encourage everyone to try new things. That's part of the fun of travel. Kids might discover to their complete surprise that they *like* frog legs or snails! At the very least, they'll probably like the implement the waiter provides for them to hold the shell while

---

Flour Power

The author of the words "a loaf of bread, a jug of wine," was a twelfth-century Persian named Omar Khayyam, but he ought to be an honorary Frenchman. Nobody takes their bread and wine more seriously.

You'll find dozens of sorts of bread in a boulangerie—a bakery. Best-known are the long, thin baguettes, but bread lovers should try pain noir, a dark rye bread, fougasse, a flat herbed variety, pain d'épice, made with honey, as well as the chocolate-filled pain au chocolat, or the chewy brioche.

Before I visited Paris for the first time, I smiled at cartoons showing Frenchmen all carrying these long loaves of bread under their arms. An exaggeration, I was sure. Nope. I'll share a bit of my travel journal with you, jotted as I sat in the window of café across the street from a small bakery and watched as the parade of bread went by.

One by one, people enter the bakery and emerge a moment later with baguettes as long as their arms. Usually they're carrying just one, but one man comes out, literally, with an armload of perhaps twenty. Two men pass my table from opposite directions, each carrying a baguette and tearing off pieces to munch as they walk

they drag the snail's garlicky little body out of its hiding place.

If the weather is nice, take a table on the sidewalk and let people admire your dinner as they stroll past. Because space is limited, you may very well find yourself sharing a table with other families. We've never shared a table with another American family, but we've met nice people from France, Sweden, England, and Japan in this way.

past. Now a bicyclist, a baguette laid across her handlebars. Now an old woman with plastic sacks of groceries that must weigh as much as she does, obviously making this the last stop of her marketing...
Everybody's got bread!

Don't be surprised if your sidewalk supper is enhanced by passing street entertainers in some areas. This often takes the form of musical instruments, most frequently accordions, but we've run into everything from magicians to jazz quartets to fire jugglers. Those last made us a bit nervous, since they were rather closer than we'd have liked, but I decided that if anything bad happened, at least I'd have my dinner flambé for no extra cost.

No! Don't eat that hot dog! You want saucisses!

Ethnic food is a great value in Paris, and prices are often much lower than those in restaurants and bistros. France was once an important colonial power, and restaurants featuring the cuisine of its former spheres of influence are common, especially North African, Middle Eastern, and Southeast Asian. You'll also see large numbers of Greek, Chinese, and Italian places.

Recommendations

✔ Save money by eating breakfast and supper in your apartment and having lunch at cafés. Shop at local markets and stores like the locals, and focus on simple, easy-to-prepare meals. But dine at a restaurant or bistro at least once.

✔ Carry emergency rations for when people start to feel hungry and out-of-sorts, or stop for rich ice cream or a *crêpe chocolat.*

✔ Try a food or preparation you've never had before and keep an open mind, whether it's snails or calf's head. French chefs aren't world renowned for nothing.

✔ Eat at sidewalk tables in fine weather and enjoy the parade of people going by.

For the latest updates to *Paris for Families*, check our page
on the Web at:

www.interlinkbooks.com/parisforfamilies.html

6. Getting Around

One of the problems with big cities is that they're hard to become a part of. You visit an attraction here, see a sight there, but never really feel like you know the city... just fragments of it.

That's one reason your family will love Paris—even though it's home to more than 2 million people, it's an intimate place, accessible to visitors. I've been in places in New York, in London, in Moscow, in other big cities, that look the same—you can't tell one from the other. But nowhere in Paris is like anywhere else. It's exciting, and not just for the kids. You really feel a special sense of place. Stand long enough on the corner and a man with an armload of baguettes will walk by.

What makes it better is that not a bit of it is hard to find. Paris doesn't hide its charm in undiscovered corners (although there are plenty of cozy places). It flaunts it. As you move around Paris, try to find a place where you can't see the Eiffel Tower, or Sacré-Coeur, or Notre Dame, or the Seine. To do that, you'll have to find a narrow street with medieval buildings rising sharply on both sides. But the buildings and the brick street and the water washing down the curbs will still tell you that you're in the Marais or the Latin Quarter. Paris is always Paris.

This chapter will show you how to find your way quickly and easily to everywhere you want to go. Paris is one of the easiest cities in the world to move about in, and in a few pages you'll be an expert. What's more, Mom and Dad will have peace of mind knowing that navigating the city is easy for the older kids who want to take off for an afternoon on their own. Nothing to it. Let's go!

Basic Issues

First let's look at four things that experienced travelers think about when wandering around an unfamiliar place, things that will help keep them comfortable and pain-free.

Safety

Paris is safe. You don't have to worry about being mugged there, and violent crime is very rare and virtually never directed against tourists. There is more careful regulation of bakeries in France than of handguns in the United States, so unless you're concerned about being bludgeoned with a stale baguette, you shouldn't fear for your safety in Paris.

Given that fact, you still don't want to do things that are really, really stupid and invite trouble, like flashing a lot of cash in a bar, then walking alone down a dark alleyway after midnight. Behavior like that might be enough to get you mugged in the Vatican! Just be yourself, don't go places that feel unsafe to you, and don't hang out in seedy areas.

The biggest crimes you have to remain alert for are pick-pocketing and bag-snatching. Men should keep their wallets in their side pockets, not in the back. Women shouldn't let purses dangle from their hands or set them down in stores or restaurants; use purses with straps that can go over your shoulder and keep them on your lap when you sit down. Protect your cameras and daypacks the same way.

But Paris police are very efficient. I happened to witness a bag-snatching on one trip to Paris, and was, in fact, almost trampled by the thief and the pursuing policeman. The chase ended quickly: The crook ran straight into the arms of four police officers walking down the street. The guy was on the ground and handcuffed before he knew what had happened.

Daypacks

When you're out and about, it's handy to be able to carry more with you than will fit into your pockets: map, camera, an extra roll or two of film, a bottle of water, a granola bar, a guidebook, maybe a dictionary or phrase book, a small notebook—the list can be as long as you like... and that's before you even start to buy souvenirs. A good daypack handles all that.

Kids are used to carrying backpacks, so bring them along. Stuffed full they make reasonable carry-on bags anyway, so they serve double duty. A large purse with a strap that goes over the shoulder, a nylon briefcase with a shoulder strap—all these are suitable.

Shoes

Don't skimp here: You want comfortable, lightweight walking shoes, sturdy and watertight. Excellent, featherlight shoes are easy to find now. You hear much about how wearing athletic shoes mark you as a tourist. That's not entirely true. Parisians wear them, but not as often, not usually stark white, and not usually to restaurants. But they do wear them out walking the dog and running errands, and people who claim otherwise may be a bit too sophisticated for their own good. It's true that some businesses disapprove of them, and a very few won't allow them. And it might also be true that a large percentage of running shoes *are* on the feet of tourists.

Frankly, I've found lightweight walking shoes in dress-shoe style that are far more comfortable and far easier on my feet than anything else I've ever tried. And that's what is most important. You'll be on your feet a lot, so choose shoes that have good support and wear well. *Don't* bring new shoes. A vacation is no place to break them in! Have at least two pairs. Changing shoes at the end of a sightseeing day, before you go out for the evening, will make your feet less tired.

Maps

Some cities offer excellent free or inexpensive maps through their tourist agencies. Readers of *London for Families* know that London is such a place. Paris, alas, is not. You can get a free map from the Paris Tourism Office, but it would be much more useful with less advertising and fewer lists of attractions. It's helpful mostly as a general guide, certainly worth having, but it omits far too many streets to be useful for really finding your way.

Almost every news kiosk in Paris stocks the *Plan de Paris* in several sizes. It's inexpensive and has all the detail you could want. But I especially like the Michelin *Paris Atlas* (No. 11 in the Michelin series) which has large, easy to use views of every street and byway, a comprehensive index, addresses for everything from churches to hospitals, expanded maps of key areas, and clear labeling in French, English, German, and Spanish. Any bookstore that doesn't stock it can get it for you quickly.

Public Transportation

Why would you even want to own a car in Paris? They are hard to park, expensive to operate, and subject to being stuck in traffic jams that extend to the horizon. Meanwhile, a few meters beneath your feet, people zip comfortably through the Metro, leaving you and your car lagging far behind.

The public transport system, the RATP, consists of the Metro (the subway or underground system), the RER (express subways and suburban rail), and buses. The network uses a single system of tickets, which are valid on any of the three types of transport. All the prices and travel below refer to central Paris, the 20 arrondissements within the Périphérique. Travel into the suburbs, unless you do a great deal of it, is best bought in single-ticket purchases.

The system is so easy to use that you'll have it mastered in a single trip. That's a comfort for parents, because the kids will be as proficient in using it as any Parisian by the end of your first day. If you decide to split up sometimes, Mom and Dad can have confidence that the kids will have no trouble finding where they want to go—and getting back! Here's your primer on public transportation in Paris.

The Metro

This is the essential way of getting around the city—its subway or underground. The Paris Metro is one of the cleanest and quietest subways in the world: The trains actually run on *rubber tires.* Service is frequent, often every two to four minutes. Stations are

You can't get lost in the Metro

clean and well-lit, although they can be difficult for someone with mobility problems, since most are accessible only by stairs.

The Metro network is extensive, with more than 200km (124 miles) of tracks and more than 300 stations. In central Paris you're never more than 500m (550 yards) from a metro station. Trains run from about 5:30 in the morning until shortly after midnight. Transfers from one of the fourteen Metro lines to another are simple, well-marked, and free. It's by far the fastest and easiest way to get from one part of Paris to another.

> *Tip:* *A common scam in busy Metro stations, especially those in railway stations, is for a person to approach you with an offer of tickets at 5F each. Don't buy them. These are used tickets, picked up off the floor, and new visitors don't recognize the cancellation marks. Buy your tickets only from the ticket booth or from a machine.*

Access is by ticket fed into a turnstile, which validates the ticket, opens the barrier, and returns your ticket to you. *Always* keep your ticket with you. Some stops require it to be fed through a turnstile again to leave the station, and the RATP has inspectors on many trains checking for valid tickets. If you don't have one, you'll be fined 100F on the spot, and no excuses will be accepted.

A single ticket on the Metro costs 8F, (€1.22 or $1.47) but there are many ways to travel more cheaply. The Metro has a number of reduced-rate options, and even experienced travelers debate which one is best. Special passes can seldom be purchased from machines; you'll have to stand in line for the ticket agent. But some *Tabacs* (tobacconists) who display the RATP sign sell tickets and carnets. There's no need to buy any of these passes before you get to Paris. They're cheaper in Paris because any other agent you buy from abroad will add a hefty service charge. Buying them is easy at any Metro station.

The Carnet: This is a packet of ten regular tickets, sold for 55F (€8.38 or $10) from ticket agents or automatic machines in virtually all stations. Tickets can be used any time, and by any member of the family—you can share your tickets, even save them for use on your next trip; they'll still be valid. For most people, the carnet is probably the most flexible option, especially if you plan to do a little walking. Even better, children between ages 4 and 10 can ride at half price. You can buy a carnet of half-price tickets (ask for *demi-tarif*) from the agent at any station, but avoid rush hours, when the line at the ticket booth can be a long one. Children under 4 ride free.

If you buy one of the following passes you will get a ticket that looks very similar to the regular one-use tickets above. But don't lose this one: It's valid for the length of time you've paid for, and is used each time you enter the station.

Mobilis Pass: If you plan to do a lot of travel on a single day, this is your best bet. This one-day pass is good for unlimited use of the RATP system and costs 30F (€4.57 or $5.46). This is good value if you expect to take four or more Metro or bus rides that day. If you've been to Paris before, this is the pass once known as the *Formula 1*.

Carte Orange: This pass is available by the week or month. The weekly pass is good for Monday through Sunday (not any seven consecutive days) or for the calendar month *only*. For this pass you need a passport-size photo. There are photo machines in many Metro stations, and they sometimes work. Bring your own. The photo is affixed to an identification card, on which you print your name, and the number of the card is written on the ticket you'll be given. This ticket is what you use to enter the Metro gates. Keep the ID card for use when you buy the pass again next week—or on your visit next year.

A weekly pass costs 82F (€12.50 or $14.92), much less than the price of two regular-fare rides per day. For a weekly pass, ask for a *coupon hebdomadaire*. The monthly pass is called a *coupon mensuel* and costs 279F (€42.54 or $50.78), a terrific value for long stays.

The drawback to both these passes is that they're not transferable. You can buy a carnet of tickets and hand them around to everyone. Each person must have his or her *own* pass, however. It's probably worth it if you're staying for a week or more, and can buy a pass on Monday or Tuesday.

Paris Visite: RATP pushes this pass hard and even sells it at the tourist bureau offices. You can buy passes good for from one to five days at prices of 55F to 175F. The passes are good for unlimited central Paris travel, like the Mobilis Pass, and supposedly has other benefits, like museum admissions. This pass is best avoided. It costs more than the Mobilis and the discounts are mostly to museums that are of little interest to families—or most other people, it seems. You can see the benefits spelled out on the RATP website and if it looks like it includes things you want to do, go ahead and buy the pass. Most families are better off with one of the other approaches.

Tip: No one is sure why, but lately a few ticket agents have told visitors the Carte Orange is only available to residents, not tourists. This is not true! It's available to anyone with 82F and a photo. Your chances of having a problem are very small but if you do, insist on seeing a supervisor. Alternatively, remember there's another station no more than 500 meters away.

Using the Metro: A map of the Metro is essential for everyone from lifelong Parisians to newly arrived visitors. You'll find it on the map you get from the Paris Tourist Office, but the first time you use the Metro or RER, ask for a free pocket-sized *Petit Plan de Paris* for each member of your family who might be traveling alone. The *Petit Plan* has good maps of the Metro, the RER, and the bus system.

Metro lines are numbered 1 through 14 and color coded on the map. At the end of each line is clearly printed the line number and the final station. That's all the information you need. To find your way, just look at your map for the nearest Metro station, then the station

nearest to your destination. If they're on the same line, it's very easy: Just get on the train headed that way. In the station, the platforms and directional signs *always* give the name of the last station on the line the train is headed for, reading *Direction*, followed by the station. You can't get on the wrong train. Just follow the *Direction* signs to the right platform.

If you have to change lines, there's still no problem. The word *Correspondance* means "connection." On your map, follow the line you're on to where it connects with a line that goes to your destination. Take note of the number of the line you want to switch to, and the *Direction* of your destination—the last station on that line. When you get to the connecting station, get off the train and look for a sign that says *Correspondance*, followed by the line number and *Direction*. Follow the signs to your platform. Do it once, and it will be automatic from then on.

The RER

The RER operates just like the Metro in central Paris, usually running deeper below ground. There's no charge to transfer from one kind of train to the other, and the tickets from your carnet or pass are good on either. There are five lines, A, B, C, D, and E that may branch off in separate directions (e.g. B2, B3, B4, etc.) once they reach the suburbs.

In central Paris there is no branching, though. Ride the RER here just like the Metro. The advantage is that there are fewer stops and the train travels faster, so it's much quicker to get from one side of Paris to the other on the RER. Your *Petit Plan* includes the central Paris RER system on the Metro map, and has a separate map of the full RER system that includes all suburbs.

The RER is the most convenient way of getting to the airports, to places like Versailles, and has even been extended to Disneyland Paris. To use the RER for out of town attractions, just tell the ticket agent your destination. As on the Metro, hang onto your ticket.

Because the lines branch off in different directions outside central Paris, make sure you get on the right train. As a train approaches, a lighted signboard above the track will tell you which stations the oncoming train will stop at. Also, the front of the train displays its final stop, and you can see on your *Petit Plan* which branch of the line that is. Simple!

Buses

You can use the same tickets you bought for the Metro and RER for the bus system. For single-use tickets like those in the carnet, just put them in the canceling machine as you enter the bus and keep the ticket with you in case an inspector turns up. If you have one of the special passes described above, however, *don't* put it in the machine; just show it to the driver. If you put it in the canceling machine, it won't work in the Metro any more.

You can also buy bus-only tickets from the driver as you board. Cancel them in the same way.

There's a bus map on your *Petit Plan*, and most bus stops in central Paris are clearly marked with maps of where the bus goes. Most tourists don't realize that, with a few exceptions, the number of the bus serves as a shorthand for where it's headed. Buses numbered in the 20s are generally headed for the Gare Saint-Lazare area. Most buses in the 30s are going to Gare de l'Est. The 40s are Gare du Nord, the 70s are Hôtel de Ville, and the 90s Montparnasse.

If you'd like to do some sightseeing by bus, try Route 72.

The bus leaves from the Hôtel de Ville and rolls past the Palais Royal, through the Place de la Concorde, and along the Seine to the Trocadéro across from the Eiffel Tower. No. 84 begins at the Panthéon and wanders through the Left Bank, has a good view of Invalides out the left side, across the Seine, past the Madeleine and ends at the Bois de Boulogne. No. 73 begins at the Musée d'Orsay, crosses the river at Concorde, and goes up the Champs Élysées to the Arc de Triomphe. Actually, it's hard to find a boring bus route.

Most buses stop running between 8 and 9 PM, but if you're out after the Metro closes, there is a system of night buses, called Noctambus that runs hourly between 1 and 5 AM (every 30 minutes on Friday and Saturday) to all of greater Paris. This is rarely something families make use of, but if you think you might need it, maps are available in Metro stations. The fare is 30F per person. A taxi might be cheaper.

Taxis

Taxis in this chapter have the same major drawback they did in Chapter 4—They usually won't take more than three people. It takes more than two chapters to change that. Taxis can be useful though, in some conditions:
- You're a family of three
- You (or a child) are hopelessly lost
- You're just too weary to go one more step
- It's very late at night.
In that case, perhaps a taxi *is* the answer.

You'll find taxis gathered at official taxi ranks all over Paris—near railway and RER stations, hotels and tourist attractions, outside important buildings and major stores. Officially, a taxi doesn't have to pick you up if you're within 50 meters of a taxi rank, but most will. As a taxi approaches, put out your arm—the universal way of hailing a taxi. If the sign on the roof is lit, though, somebody hailed him before you did.

Tourists generally don't have to worry about being cheated by Paris taxis. Look at your map and notice the route the driver is taking. You should be able to go anywhere in inner Paris, arrondissements 1 through 7, for under 100F, unless traffic is horrendous. That's true even at night, when there's a surcharge to the fare.

If you're not sure your French is up to the task, have your address written on a piece of paper, including the postcode (the 5-digit number beginning with 75), which will tell the driver which arrondissement you live in. The accepted tip is 10 percent of the fare showing on the meter.

On foot

Our favorite way to see a city, though, is the old fashioned way. We walk. Only by spending as much time as possible walking can you duck into little courtyards and narrow streets, almost unseen from the thorough-fare... or peer into shop windows as you pass... or change direction on the spur of the moment when something catches your eye... or, when you've walked your limit, have a perfect opportunity to relax in a park or at a cheerful sidewalk table and order a cup of coffee or cold drink to cheer you while your feet rest.

When we go somewhere new, we like to orient ourselves by walking past as many landmark places as we have the legs for. Bus tours don't do it for us, because sites are more disconnected. We see the famous buildings but don't get much of a feel for where they are in relation to each other. Besides, it's a great way to stretch our legs after hours of travel.

The Lain Walking Tour of Central Paris

Paris is tough. We can take you on a nice, more-or-less circular tour of highlights in many cities—New York, London, Boston, Washington, and others. The highlights of Paris lay pretty much in a straight line, though, mostly along the Seine. Any *walking* tour will inevitably leave things out. But which do you leave out of a Paris walk: The Eiffel Tower or Notre Dame? Yet they're at opposite ends of central Paris.

But just stick with your intrepid host for a few pages more. There's a solution or two. The route we're about to cover runs a bit over 8km—roughly 5 miles. That's certainly not too far to walk. When we travel we often walk twice that far each day. If it's a pleasant day, this is a good way to spend it—strolling easily along the route, not marching relentlessly. But if your children are small, a walk as long as this might not be practical. Or you might simply prefer not to walk that far. That's OK. You're on vacation and are supposed to be having fun, not trying to train for the triathalon. I've never had a desire to behave like a drill sergeant.

First, you can easily break the walk into two or three parts, and might have to when you get distracted by something you want to spend much more time with. That might be the best way to approach it, after all. You'll be going past a lot of great stuff. Second, it's easy to opt out at any time. The walk goes past, or within a block of, twenty Metro stations. When you get tired of walking, head home for a rest, or branch off in another direction. Third, you can hop on a bus

You won't need to hitch a ride to get around

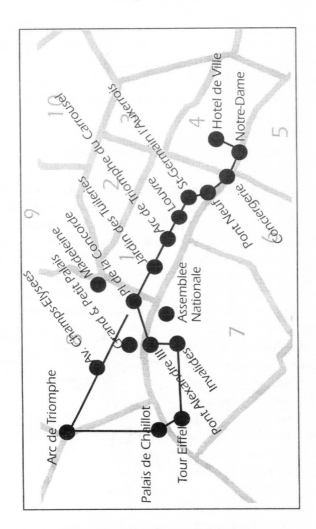

The Lain Walking Tour

when you're tired. I'll tell you which ones are going the same way we are. As we walk, I'll point out some highlights and tell you the chapters where they are discussed in more detail. When you look for street signs, look on the sides of buildings. So—are you ready? Then tighten your shoelaces and let's go!

Stage 1—Cité to the Louvre: Let's start where Paris started, the Ile de la Cité, one of a pair of islands in the Seine here. This is where the Parisii built their settlement 2,000 years ago, where the conquering Romans settled, where the city grew from. Take the Metro to Cité (Line 4) and when you climb up the steps leading out of the station, you'll see the towers of **Notre Dame** (Ch. 12). Well, here's our first stop and we're already tempted by an attractive catalog of diversions. Shall we go in? Climb the towers? Investigate the park behind? Indulge yourself if you want: Paris will wait for you. When you leave, walk down the street that leaves the plaza on your left as you face the church. You'll cross the Seine here on the Pont d'Arcole. Cross the busy street on the other side of the bridge and walk up to the ornate building straight ahead, the **Hôtel de Ville** (Ch. 10), the city hall.

Retrace your steps toward the river, re-cross the street, but don't go back over the bridge. Just walk along the river. You're on the Quai de Gesvres, one of the picturesque quais that line the river. They're ideal for walking. As you stroll, notice the turreted building on the island. That's the **Conciergerie** (Ch. 11), once a palace and an infamous prison, and still a courthouse. The bridge here, or rather, its predecessor, the Pont au Change, is where moneylenders had their headquarters 800 years ago. In those days the bridge was so cluttered with buildings you couldn't see the river as you crossed.

The next bridge is the **Pont Neuf** (Ch. 10), which means "new bridge." Actually, it's the oldest bridge in Paris. Cross the street here by the department store La Samaritaine, past the Panorama café, to Rue de l'Amiral de Coligny. On the right is the church St-

Germain l'Auxerrois (Ch. 12). But cross the street in front of the church and go through the entrance in the grand colonnade. You're in the **Louvre** (Ch. 13). The courtyard here is certainly beautiful, but when you pass through the opposite archway, you'll see the spectacular glass pyramid that covers the underground entrance to the museum. This is another place we're tempted to linger, but if you want to walk on, there's much more to see.

If that's enough walking for now, you're near the Palais Royal/Louvre Metro (Lines 1, 7).

Stage 2—The Louvre to Ponte Alexandre III: As you walk through the broad plaza you'll come to a triumphal arch built by Napoléon, the **Arc de Triomphe du Carrousel**, impressive enough until you see another arch near the end of the walk. Go through the arch and stroll through the gardens here, the **Jardin des Tuileries** (Ch. 14). There was once a royal palace here, too. Watch the children sailing boats in the fountains and walk all the way to the end of the gardens. The building at the end, on your left, is the **Musée de l'Orangerie** (Ch. 13), devoted to impressionist painting. If you go up the embankment here, you have a splendid view of the **Place de la Concorde** (Ch. 11) with the ancient Egyptian **Obelisk** in its center. From here you can look straight down the **Champs Élysées** (Ch. 16) to the Arc de Triomphe. We'll be there in a little while.

Go back down the embankment and into the Place de la Concorde. (Before you do, there are public toilets just inside the gate if anyone would like to stop a moment.) Turn left and walk toward the river and stroll along the quai. As you walk, look through the Place de la Concorde. At the end of the street you'll see the church of St. Mary Magdalene, usually just called **La Madeleine** (Ch. 10, 16), looking like a Greek temple. Look across the river to your left and you'll see **Assemblée Nationale** (Ch. 10), home of the French parliament. But walk on, to the ornate **Petit Palais** (Ch. 10) and **Grand Palais** (Ch. 10, 15) on your right, great exhibition halls built for a world's fair early in the last century. On your left is the **Pont Alexandre III** (Ch. 10), a beautiful and fanciful bridge.

Shortcut: If you want to save the Eiffel Tower for another time, walk through the Place de la Concorde (with the lights! Traffic is frantic!) and stroll along the Avenue des Champs Élysées to the Arc de Triomphe, a pleasant walk of about 1km. Or you can catch a No. 73 bus here that will take you directly to the Arc. The Invalides Metro (Line 8, RER C) is on the Left Bank end of the bridge.

Stage 3—Pont Alexandre III to the Eiffel Tower: If you're tired of walking but want to go to the Eiffel Tower, you can skip the next part of the walk and catch a No. 72 bus here that will take you directly across the Seine from the tower. It's up to you. But if you're still in the mood to walk with me, cross the bridge here. Now you're at **Invalides** (Ch. 11), where Napoléon built his rest home for old soldiers and where he, himself, is entombed. The building now also houses the **Musée de l'Armée** (Ch. 15). Walk down the center of the gorgeous green Esplanade. Stroll straight ahead until you get to the low wall before the entrance to the museum. Just to the right is an absolutely stunning view of the Eiffel Tower. That's where we're headed.

At the wall, bear right, past the Metro entrance, down the Avenue de la Motte Picquet. You'll cross a wide, busy intersection and the great complex of buildings on your left is the **École Militaire**, the French military academy. From in front of this school you can see one of the world's most sumptuous pieces of eye candy. Now you're looking down the green expanse of the **Champ de Mars** with the **Eiffel Tower** (Ch. 12) looming above. It's probably bigger, more massive, than you imagined, an impression that will grow as you walk along the paths toward it— massive, but curiously delicate with its iron lacework.

Do we linger here? The temptation is almost too much to resist. I'll wait in the park and rest my feet if you'd like to go up in the Tower. *The Bir-Hakeim Metro (Line 6) is here.*

Stage 4—Eiffel Tower to Concorde: Now we'll cross under the Tower and walk across the bridge toward the striking white building on the other side of the Seine, the **Palais de Chaillot** (Ch. 15). Built for another world's fair in the 1930s, the building has the loveliest fountains in Paris, an incredible view of the Eiffel Tower, and several fascinating museums. Walk through the plaza in the center and go around the traffic circle at the Place du Trocadéro to the second street counter clockwise. This is the Avenue Kléber. The walk isn't too long and it's a fine street, but there's nothing especially noteworthy here, so let's catch a No. 22 or 30 bus to the **Arc de Triomphe** (Ch. 10), the great triumphal arch begun by Napoléon. Here we can visit the grave of the unknown soldier, climb the arch, or just watch in rapt amazement the traffic converging on this circle from twelve different streets!

It's time to head back now. This would be a good time for a stroll down the famous **Avenue des Champs-Élysées** (Ch. 16), or a ride on a No. 73 bus, back down to the Place de la Concorde to the Metro.

We haven't seen all of Paris—not by any means! But we've done a lot of cherry-picking on this walk, and gotten some great photos. Now we can sit down and rest our weary legs a while and talk about money in the next chapter.

Recommendations

✔ Take comfortable, well broken-in shoes with good support. You'll spend much more time on your feet than usual.

✔ Most tourists are content with the Metro but don't forget the bus. It's slower but a lot more scenic.

✔ Walk as much as you can. You'll see more, be surprised more often, and get more personal with Paris.

7. *Speaking Francly*

The challenge of learning to think in another currency system is almost as great as that of learning to handle another language. In many ways, in fact, talking about finances *is* another language. It certainly seems that way, at least, when I'm talking to my accountant! But travelers, take courage! Even the French have to go through the process of learning a new financial language—in their own country!

This chapter needs to deal with two different systems of currency, because everything changes in 2002. On January 1 of that year, the new euro coins and notes begin circulating in eleven European countries belonging to the European Economic and Monetary Union (EMU). And on July 1, 2002, the national currencies of those nations—the French franc, the German mark, the Spanish peseta, the Italian lira, and others—cease to exist. Since the beginning of 1999, international bookkeeping has been done in euros, and prices have been posted in euros alongside amounts in national currencies.

So *everybody* has had to learn a new system, not just people from outside France. The difference is that after July 1, 2002, no one from the eleven countries adopting the euro will have to learn another currency when they visit any other nation in that group.

No matter where you're from, though, it won't take you much time to catch on to the system. For the first day or two you'll count your change carefully. After that you'll glance at it and drop it in your pocket the way you do at home. For three or four days you'll do loads of mental arithmetic every time you make a purchase or pay a restaurant bill, calculating how much that is in pounds or dollars or yen. After that, you'll just pay it without thinking because you've got a handle on relative values. It always turns out to be simpler than you expect.

Two Currency Systems

Let's just outline the two currency systems you might encounter, depending on when you arrive. Only those visiting France before July 1, 2002, will have to know both.

The French System

The national currency of France has been the French *franc*, usually indicated by one *F* behind the numeral—although sometimes it's two F's. There is no separate symbol like $ or £ or ¥. The franc is divided into 100 smaller units called *centimes*.

Notes (Americans call them *bills*) are different sizes, following the usual European convention of larger notes for larger amounts. You'll find notes in the denominations of 20F, 50F, 100F, 200F, and 500F. If denominations went any higher, the notes would be large enough to wear as scarves. Notes are easy to distinguish, too, because each denomination is a different color. You won't mistake them; the denomination is written in huge numbers. Portraits are of famous men and women of France, and refreshingly, not one is a politician! The French are a highly civilized people.

There are coins of numerous denominations in circulation. You will see:

20F—large bimetal with gold color outside, silver color inside, brass plug in the middle
10F—small bimetal with gold outside, silver inside
5F—large silver-colored
2F—smaller silver-colored, rough milled edge
1F—slightly smaller silver-colored, fine milled edge
½F—small silver colored
20c—large brass colored
10c—medium brass colored
5c—small brass colored

You might also run into a few older coins, especially the old 10F piece, a very large copper coin.

There's no doubt, I'm afraid, that at some point you *will* give a shopkeeper 20c thinking it's 20F, and wonder why he's standing there expectantly instead of making change. It's OK— he's used to it. Take heart: When euros begin circulating, he'll have to puzzle over the coinage in his own country, so forgive him his scowl for now.

The Conversion Factor

While exchange rates among world currencies fluctuate hourly, currencies of EMU countries are permanently fixed against the euro. The permanent exchange rate is 1F = €6.55.

The European System

If you're coming from another country in the EMU, things are much easier... once you learn the new system yourself! But at the beginning, everyone has to learn it. The monetary unit is called the *euro*, indicated by the symbol € before the numeral. The euro is divided into 100 smaller units called cents.

Euro notes follow the usual European pattern of different-colored notes that grow in size as the denomination grows larger. The notes feature pictures of rather generic-looking windows, bridges, and gates that are supposed to look somehow European. You'll have to judge that for yourself. Some notes have had to be redesigned because the bridges they were based on were too recognizable.

Euro notes come in the following denominations and colors: €5 (gray), €10 (red), €20 (blue), €50 (orange), €100 (green), €200 (yellow-brown), and €500 (pink).

You'll find eight coins in circulation, all with very large, clear numbers indicating the denomination on the front, along with a design showing outlines of the EMU nations. The nations get closer together as the denominations get larger, until they are blended together on the largest coins. The backs of the coins have designs representing individual member nations. The larger coins

You'll soon get used to the many types of coins

represent larger denominations, except for the copper 5-cent coin, which is slightly larger than the silver-colored 10-cent coin. The coins are:

€2—bimetal with silver color outside, gold color inside
€1—bimetal with gold color outside, silver color inside
50 cents—gold color, rough milled edge
20 cents—gold color; "Spanish Flower" shape (round with seven indentations around the edge)

10 cents—gold color, rough milled edge
5 cents—copper color, smooth edge, slightly larger than 10-cent
2 cents—copper color, grooved edge
1 cent—copper color, smooth edge, smallest coin

It won't take long to catch on. Even the kids will adapt quickly—probably before the parents do, as a matter of fact!

Four Types of Money

In simpler times, you didn't have to think about how to pay. You just wore a leather purse at your belt jammed with as many gold coins as you could carry, mounted your horse, and set off on your travels. Things are more complicated now, and if you tried to spend a gold coin in a shop, no one would take it—few shopkeepers have probably ever seen a gold coin.

Travelers must balance up to four ways of handling their finances. There's no agreement on which way is best. If you ask four experienced travelers for advice, you're sure to get five firm opinions on the subject. In fact, some sort of a mix is best. Let's look at the options.

Cash

This is the easiest method: pay as you go in cash. But nobody wants to carry thousands of francs on vacation; it isn't wise and it isn't safe. Yet many places will accept *only* cash. The use of credit cards isn't universal, and it's silly (or impossible) to charge small purchases. Just try to buy a 3F newspaper with a credit card and see the reception you get! So cash is a necessity. And it will have to be in francs or euros. That newspaper vendor will be no more willing to accept dollars, yen, or anything else, than a newspaper vendor in Atlanta or Osaka will accept francs or euros. You'll have to convert *yours* to *theirs*.

If you're coming from another EMU country in 2002 or later, you have no worries about converting your own currency to something you can use—you use the same thing. But for the rest of us, we worry: *Will I get a better exchange rate at home or in France?*

There's no certain answer.

I've almost always found better rates at home than I've seen posted abroad, but I've occasionally found a rate abroad that was 1 or 2 percent better than I'd received. At home, at least, I have time to check all my local banks and see who's giving the best rate. I don't want to have to spend time on my holiday doing that once I get abroad. Any slight difference I've found so far has been less than my time is worth, so I've decided that, for this traveler, it's best to get the cash I want to take *before* leaving home.

It's a good idea to take as much cash as you'll need for the first day or two. It's no fun to have to stop in the long line at the currency window at the airport (a guaranteed terrible exchange rate) when you arrive, or to try to find a bank or cash machine your first afternoon in Paris. No matter how we plan to mix the other types of money, we always carry a supply of cash that will last a couple of days. Trains, buses, taxis almost always insist on cash, and even when you *can* use a credit card (the ticket window for the RER will take them, for example), cash is easier and faster.

> **Tip:** The one place you should never *exchange money is at your hotel. The rate you get will inevitably be the worst* rate you could ever find—10 or even 20 percent worse than any bank in town.

Most banks and bureaux de change post their rates. But each might also impose a service charge that is not posted. That has the effect of worsening the exchange rate you get. Overall, it might be a better idea to buy cash before leaving home so you can do it at your leisure, not when you're suddenly pressed for money. Before a trip, we keep an eye on the exchange rates and try to buy when the rate looks most favorable. In practice that's usually not necessary because the amount of cash is relatively small, no more than a thousand francs or so. Most of our money is in other forms.

Traveler's Checks

There was a time that we took nearly all our money in the form of traveler's checks. Traveler's checks have the wonderful advantage over cash of being replaceable if they're lost or stolen—something that hasn't happened to us yet... but it isn't wise to get complacent. Traveler's checks are still an excellent way to carry money, especially if you keep two things in mind:

First, get them in francs. If you get them in your own currency you still have to trust to the exchange rate abroad and have the dual problem of not only getting them cashed but also converted. Transactions are cheaper, faster, and easier when they're in francs.

Second, watch fees and exchange rates. One reason we like traveler's checks is because we're members of an auto club that sells them at an exchange rate about 10 percent lower than banks sell cash, and charges no transaction fee. The rate is outstanding and we take full advantage of it. You might belong to an auto club, credit union, bank, or building association that does the same thing.

It's true that once in Paris you must find a place to cash the checks. Almost any bank or bureau de change will do that, and some won't even charge a fee. In addition, if the checks are from American Express or Thomas Cook, you'll have no problem finding a Paris office of the company where they'll be cashed free. Each has several locations in Paris.

North American visitors take note: In the United States and Canada, traveler's checks are accepted as payment in most restaurants and retail stores. That is *not* true in Paris. The number of establishments that will take traveler's checks, even those in francs, is vanishingly small. You'll have to cash them. That's the way we operate, in fact, keeping enough currency for a couple of days, and just cashing traveler's checks two or three times a week when it's convenient.

Debit Cards

These aren't credit cards, although they look like them. You might call them cashpoint cards, bank cards, or ATM cards. You can use them to get money from a cash machine or to pay for purchases or meals like a credit card. The difference is that the money is immediately deducted from your bank account back home, instead of being billed later like a credit card.

There are real advantages to this. The exchange rate is the best you're likely to get anywhere, because you're normally charged the bank rate, rather than the higher consumer rate. There are machines all over town so you can usually get some quick cash when you need it and you don't have to worry about carrying a lot of money or cashing traveler's checks.

But there are no unmixed blessings.

Things can go wrong. If a cash machine eats your card, it can be time-consuming to get it back, especially if your French is less than fluent. You'll get it back eventually, but you could be several days without it. Also, you have to plan before you leave to have plenty of money in your account back home. When you take 500F from the cash machine, you have no way of knowing exactly how much your bank is charging you. People do, occasionally, drain their accounts at home and suddenly find that a cash machine is refusing to give them money—probably just when they need it most. You also may have to pay a fee to your bank for each transaction, something that, in effect, hikes up your exchange rate a bit. You can check on that before you leave home.

Those things haven't happened to me (yet) but one problem has, two or three times. Cash machines are often behind glass doors that are locked on evenings and weekends. The bank's own customers can open the doors with their own cards, but no one else can. Over the years, I've spent a couple of worried hours looking for a machine I could get access to, usually just ending up standing next to a locked door looking impoverished until someone was willing to let me in. I've never actually failed to get needed money, but I'd be glad to show you which gray hairs came from worrying about it.

Otherwise it's a good system. You do need to make sure that the PIN number for your card has four numbers—that's all that will work in Paris—and that the machine you want to use is on the same cash machine system as your card. There should be stickers near the machines and logos on the back of your card. *Plus* and *Cirrus* are the most common. Debit cards make it possible to get emergency cash, and even to take less along with you. I'm not at the point yet where I'm willing to rely solely on them (although many people do) but they are a great convenience and I use them more each time I travel.

Credit Cards

The fourth type of money you can use isn't *your* money at all, it's somebody else's: your credit card. You can use all major international cards in Paris. Not everywhere takes them, but large (or expensive) stores, restaurants, and hotels invariably will. Their only drawback is similar to that

It's silly to charge everything you buy

with debit cards: You don't know exactly how much you've spent until you get the bill. The exchange rate changes each day. But the ups and downs will probably even out. Again, the exchange rate you're charged is the more favorable bank-to-bank rate.

Because several readers of *London for Families* e-mailed the question, let's cover one more possible type of payment method: personal checks in your own currency drawn on a bank in your country. Forget it.

How Much Money Will I Need?

This is one of the most popular questions of all, and no travel writer, travel agent, banker, or advisor can answer. The worksheets in Chapter 20 will help you come close, though. We always budget on the high side when we travel, on the theory that it's better to come home with leftover money than to run out before we're finished enjoying ourselves. We don't think they have debtors' prisons in France any more, but who wants to take the chance?

We budget high and make sure we have at least 10 percent more money available than we budget. We're actually pretty frugal when we travel, the only way, really, that a couple of teachers could consider taking the whole family abroad. We've always come home with extra money—more than enough to pay for developing all our film... and there's always a lot of *that*.

Carrying Your Money

In Chapter 3, you probably caught a reference to buying a money belt or neck pouch for carrying your treasury. This is a good time to remind you. Every year tourists find themselves jostled in a crowd or surrounded by a boisterous group of children, laughing and playing. Only later, back in their room or when the bill comes in the restaurant do they learn the awful truth—their money is gone!

This won't happen to you... certainly not if you're prepared. But while muggers are rare in Europe, pickpockets are not. The basic rule: *Never carry more money in your wallet or purse than you expect to use that day.* That's the traveler's creed, and you violate it at your peril. But what to do with the rest? Leaving it in a hotel room is seldom a good idea. Just carry it with you.

Any outdoor outfitter or travel store will stock a lightweight nylon money belt that will probably cost no more than the average lunch. It's the best investment you can make. Worn under your trousers or skirt, it's invisible and comfortable. You'll forget you're wearing it fifteen minutes after you put it on. In your wallet, carry the money you expect to need for the day, as well as a credit or bank card. Keep the rest of your cash and traveler's checks, and an emergency credit card, in the money belt. If you find that you need more money, you can retrieve more from the belt with a quick trip into the toilet.

If it's more comfortable, you can get a neck pouch instead for the same thing. Tucked under your shirt or blouse, it's inaccessible to someone who thinks he has a better use for your money than you do. The zippered "fanny packs" or "bum bags" that so many tourists wear outside their clothes don't provide anywhere near the same level of security that the belt or pouch afford; they're awfully easy to slice off in a crowd, and even easier to burgle than your pocket.

Recommendations

✔ Take a mix of money—cash, traveler's checks, debit cards, and credit cards for the most flexibility.

✔ Convert your money to francs or euros before you leave home; you have more time to shop for the best rate.

✔ Carry enough cash to get you through the first day or two. Standing in line at the bank is a lousy way to start your holiday.

✔ Never carry more cash than you need for the day in your purse or wallet. Keep the bulk of your funds in your money belt or neck pouch.

For the latest updates to *Paris for Families*, check our page
on the Web at:

www.interlinkbooks.com/parisforfamilies.html

8. Living Like a Local

Maybe there's no more important chapter in any travel book than one like this. That's not intended to downplay the importance of the rest of the book. There's a lot of (I hope) valuable information about planning in the chapters that came before this one, and the second part of the book grazes its way cheerfully through the highlights of Paris's many attractions. But *this* chapter is different. This chapter tells you how to get the most out of your trip.

One of the biggest problems with travel is that it is done at such a frenetic, breakneck pace that it's more exhausting than staying home and going to work.

And it's very easy to go somewhere on a trip and then insulate yourself from the place you're visiting the whole time you're there. You do that by staying in name-brand hotels that are straight out of the same cookie cutter as every other one in the chain, by going nowhere but to the same tourist attractions that every other visitor sees, by using taxis to travel more than a few blocks so you don't get lost, and eating mostly at chain restaurants with familiar names.

However long you stay, you're never *a part of* the place you're visiting, always *apart from* it. It's almost like paying somebody a lot of money to let you watch a travelogue on TV about the place.

If you're going to invest so much time, money, and energy in visiting a memorable place like Paris, though, it just makes sense to squeeze as much out of the experience as you can. That's what's at the core of the Lain travel philosophy: to *Live Like a Local*, to integrate yourself as much as you can during your short stay into the daily life of the place you're visiting.

Oh, of course there's no way you can go somewhere for the first time and *not* be a tourist. But the idea is to approach the city you're visiting—your temporary home—on its own terms, instead of expecting it to conform to yours. In this era of a shrinking world, it's one of the most valuable and useful lessons children can learn: Other people's ways of doing things aren't necessarily better or worse than their own. They're just different. And we should learn about *why* they do things the way they do.

We live in a diverse world and the world today's children will inherit will probably be more diverse still. Understanding and accepting—and coping with—other ways of life is critical.

OK, sorry. Enough philosophy. But that ought to be part of the reason for a trip like this, not just to take pretty photographs. Anyway, we were talking about how to live like a local.

That's one reason this book urges you to rent an apartment for a stay of a week or more. This way you will shop in local stores, live in a residential neighborhood surrounded by Parisians, be more likely to adopt the pace of life of your hosts. It's nothing like staying in a hotel. Visitors too often see locals as just part of the local color, as characters in a vast Parisian theme park. When you live the life of a Parisian, that doesn't happen to you. (Although you should be prepared for other tourists to mistake *you* for a Parisian and see you as part of the local color. Smile and wave your baguette for the camera!)

The "Rude Parisian" Myth

There is no more pervasive piece of travel folklore than the notion that Paris is populated with rude, arrogant people who snub and intimidate tourists.

It's not true.

There are four reasons why people have this impression of Parisians. The first has to do with the notion of attitude we were discussing above. It's a maxim of travel that if you bring something with you on a trip, you're likely to find it when you arrive. This applies equally to your socks and to your preconceptions. If you or your kids *expect* Parisians to be rude, chances are almost a hundred percent that you'll find rude Parisians. Conversely, if you expect people to be friendly and helpful,

A Smattering of French

Europeans grow up surrounded, for the most part, by languages other than their own, so they are seldom intimidated by them, even if they don't speak them. But people who come from countries where a single language predominates are often terrified of going somewhere where they cannot make simple needs known and where they are, quite suddenly, illiterate. Unfortunately they usually deal with it by staying home.

Please don't put off your trip because you don't know the language; you'll miss so much! And your kids will miss a fabulous opportunity to broaden their world. You'll cope perfectly well in Paris and, despite their fearsome reputation on linguistic matters, the French will help you if you make the smallest effort.

What annoys Parisians is the way visitors come into their country and just expect the French to speak their language. Under those conditions, Parisians will sometimes stubbornly refuse to understand a visitor's language, even if they know it well. Wouldn't you think it arrogant if someone invited himself into your house and not only ignored your own way of doing things but insisted that you do everything his way? Of course! You can hardly blame a Parisian for wanting to speak his own language in his own home town.

But if you can learn just a few phrases of French (hint: practice at the dinner table so everyone can learn) things are almost sure

chances are that's exactly what you'll find. Encourage the kids to approach the trip with a sense of humor, a sense of adventure, with flexibility, and with a willingness to suspend judgment about whose way is better, theirs or the French. Attitude is everything.

Second, Paris is a big city, and like big cities everywhere, people rush, tend to be a bit brusque —or at least very direct. Paris is like any other city of more than two million people in that way—no different in any important respect from people I've met in Chicago, New York, London, Moscow, or anywhere else. Big city people are in a hurry.

The third point is a cultural one. Europeans visiting the United

to go very smoothly. If you begin an exchange with a stammered Bonjour, madam. Je suis désolé—Je parle un petit peu de français *(Good day, madam. I'm sorry—I speak very little French) you'll probably find that she switches to your language if she's able, finds someone who can, or treats you with a patience usually reserved for small children, injured pets, and polite tourists.*

Some people suggest it's because the French can't bear to hear their own language mangled as badly as tourists do. I think they're just a lot more polite than others give them credit for.

Remind your kids that you have to assume the goodness and helpfulness of people. When I enter a restaurant and greet the waiter in horrid French, he always replies cheerfully and with a barrage of words I can't possibly follow. Maybe he's asking if I'd like to sit near the window, but perhaps he's smiling while saying "American tourist, no matter what you order I'm bringing you braised camel lungs." But the service is always good, and I've always gotten a meal that looks like what I've ordered (when I've known what it was supposed to look like). I insist on trying to carry on in atrocious French (even when the waiter would rather we switch to English) and I hope, when I leave, he says to his partner, "He's terrible. But he tries."

States are sometimes a bit taken aback by the almost relentless cheerfulness of North Americans, the artificial chattiness in shops and restaurants. Most of the world isn't like that. Smiles may be fewer than some visitors are used to, but they may be more genuine when they occur.

The fourth point is an important one. If you think a Parisian has been rude to you, it's almost certainly because *you were rude first!*

Now I know that nobody who is nice enough to buy my book is a rude person. It's quite an accidental rudeness. But most visitors treat most Parisians with an unintentional rudeness the very first time they open their mouths. They omit one word— *Bonjour!*

It's such a little thing, but it's a mark of politeness in Paris, and to omit it implies to the person you're addressing that you think you're superior to him, too good to have to be polite. Listen for it among Parisians. When they walk into a bakery, stop for a newspaper, buy a Metro ticket—every exchange begins with *Bonjour, monsieur* (Good day, sir) or perhaps *Bonsoir, madam* (Good evening, madam). It's universal, and to omit it is rude. A polite *Merci, Au revoir* when you leave is also appreciated.

Even if you speak no French at all, practice these greetings religiously in every encounter. You'll be surprised, indeed

A polite "Bonjour" is appreciated by everyone

amazed, at the difference it makes. The more you know about a place and its customs, the more you'll enjoy yourself and the better you'll adapt. This is a prime example.

Daily Living

You can't possibly know as much about Paris life from reading a book as you can from being there for a few weeks, but in this section we'll cover some of the little things you might find it helpful to know, and a few little Parisian quirks you'll recognize when you've been there a few days.

Time, Temperature, and Measurement

Time is often printed on the basis of a 24-hour clock, with a period (.) as a separator, not a colon (:). Nine-thirty in the morning would be written as 9.30, while nine-thirty at night would be 21.30. If you're used to a 12-hour clock, just subtract 12.

As in most of the world, temperatures are given in France on the Celsius scale. If you're used to Fahrenheit, there's a mathematical formula for converting one scale to the other that I won't give you unless you insist. Just keep a few benchmarks in mind:

-10°C = 14°F = *frigid*
- 5°C = 23°F = *frosty*
0°C = 32°F = *freezing*
5°C = 41°F = *cold*
10°C = 50°F = *chilly*
15°C = 59°F = *cool*
20°C = 68°F = *comfortable*
25°C= 77°F = *warm*
30°C = 86°F = *hot (for Paris, at least!)*

Measurement of distances, weight, and everything else is on the metric system, a system used everywhere but the United

States. Americans will manage adequately if they remember the following:

1 meter   = a little more than 3 feet
1 kilometer = a bit over ½ mile
1 kilogram = about 2.2 pounds
1 liter   = just over 1 quart

Large numbers in France are usually separated into sets of three with periods, while a decimal is indicated with a comma, just the opposite of the way it is done in some other places. So one million francs would be written 1.000.000F while one and a half meters would be written 1,5m.

Media

If you can read French, you have Paris daily newspapers representing all corners of the political spectrum to consider. Moving politically from right to left are *Le Figaro, France Soir, Le Parisien, Le Monde, Libération,* and *L'Hamanité.* You'll find the most complete international coverage in *Le Figaro* and *Le Monde.* For local news, pick up *Le Parisien.* If you're a non-francophone, major newspapers from around the world are available at news kiosks all over the city. Best bet for speakers of English is the *International Herald Tribune,* which is a joint venture of the *New York Times* and the *Washington Post* and is printed in Paris.

If you want to know what's going on at the museums and in the theaters, pick up a copy of *Pariscope.* At 3F, it's the best bargain in town. Even if you don't read a word of French, it's easy to figure out the listings with the help of a small dictionary. There's a small English-language section in the back produced by the publishers of *Time Out,* the big London-based entertainment magazine.

French television offers six channels of entertainment ranging from silly game shows with gaudily dressed hosts to serious documentary. Films are sometimes shown in their original language, so there's a chance for you to encounter a touch of home. Many hotels and some apartment offer satellite TV packages with a larger variety of world programing. CNN is the most common English-language channel in such offerings.

Telephone

It is virtually impossible to find a coin-operated telephone in Paris any longer. To use a public phone, purchase a phone card from a *tabac*. They're sold in denominations of 50 and 120 units and cost less than 1F per unit. Pick up the receiver and slide the card, computer chip face up, into the slot on the phone. The telephone will "read" the chip to see how many units you have left on the card, and will display the number on a small screen. Then you'll get a dial tone and can call your number. When you hang up, the card will pop out of the slot.

Many public phones take standard credit cards, which is useful for making long-distance calls home. Never charge an international call to your hotel room. Most hotels put enormous mark-ups on such calls, often 100 percent or more. Use a calling card or call from a public phone.

If you've rented an apartment, your phone will probably be set so you can make only local calls from it unless you have an international calling card from a telephone company.

Dress

Paris may be the center of the fashion world, but supermodels are not exactly thick on the ground. People do dress up to go to the opera, and restaurants that carry Michelin stars expect gentlemen in jackets and ties, but otherwise, few situations call for more than what Europeans refer to as "smart casual." That means trousers without holes and that go to the shoe-tops, shirts with collars but without words, shoes that are more at home on the street than on a basketball court. Kids can be more casual still, as long as their jeans are not ragged and the writing on their shirts not offensive.

For that matter, you'll see plenty of gym shoes even on Parisians, but they're generally not white. Shorts on men are usually reserved for picnicking. Just wear neat, sensible clothes and no one will give it a second thought.

Health

Visitors from other countries in the EU have the same medical coverage they do at home. Visitors from other countries are covered for life-threatening emergency care, but must normally pay for other medical services. Save your receipts. Your own medical insurance or health care system will probably reimburse you when you get home, but it's a good idea to check before you go abroad.

If anyone in your family takes prescription medication, bring it in the original bottle from the pharmacy. If it's possible you will need more of a medication while you're abroad, make sure your prescription lists the drug by its generic name; brand names differ in other parts of the world.

Embassies keep lists of physicians who speak your language and will put you in touch with one in case of an emergency.

Animals

The French love animals and you're likely to see dogs wherever you go, even in restaurants and exclusive shops. That's heartwarming. But a problem grows from that. Now I must find a way of putting this delicately—this is a family publication, after all. The greatest danger you will face in walking the streets of Paris certainly is not being mugged. It's not the traffic (if you're careful). It's not the danger of being unable to comm-

Watch your steps on Paris streets

unicate in an emergency. It's the constant danger of putting your foot in something on the sidewalk that really shouldn't be there.

Paris is a lovely city and your eyes will eagerly rise to follow the graceful spires of churches, the stirring authority of triumphal arches, the grand sweep of the riverside. But cast an occasional eye on the humble side-walk as you stroll.

Cleanliness

That single civic foible aside, Paris is a remarkably clean city. Litter is almost non-existent, water washes through the gutters of streets almost continuously in many places, and special broom and vacuum trucks clean the streets literally from dawn to dark. Recycling bins are everywhere. My personal favorites are the ones that look like gigantic green apples with wormholes. You put glass bottles in the holes.

You'll find public toilets in museums, cafés (usually for customers only), and parks. Sometimes you'll be charged a fee of 2–3F—but it can be worth it. The plumbing is almost always modern, but there's still a chance that you'll see one of the old-fashioned squat toilets in a café, basically a private compartment with a hole in the floor and a place to put your feet. Not so bad for the males in your group but less convenient for the females. They're well on their way to extinction.

One Parisian innovation, copied now by other cities, is the public self-cleaning toilet. You see them all over the city, large silver pods set in the middle of public squares, along the streets, and in the corners of parks. Put 2F into the slot next to the green sign and the door opens. Go in, close the door, and you have about 15 minutes of privacy. If you're still there at the end of your time, the door will open anyway, so pay attention. When you leave, the door will lock and the entire cubical will be spray-cleaned and disinfected before the light turns green again. They're a great convenience.

If only they would make them for dogs.

Recommendations

✔ Before your trip, talk a lot about the importance of attitude and flexibility. Nothing is more important for a successful trip. Enjoy the differences, don't criticize them. If you wanted everything to be just like home, you'd stay there. This is the most important of all the recommendations in the book.

✔ Learn at least a few French phrases. It's polite, and will be appreciated.

✔ Always carry a few 2F coins when you go out.

✔ Watch your step.

Part II
The Best of Paris

Part I focused on planning for the trip, and survival skills in Paris itself. Part II shows you what you came for—the sights of Paris. Of course you couldn't see *everything* in the city unless you moved here for ten years, so this section has left out a few things. What it includes, though, is the best that Paris offers for *families*, the exciting and memorable places that will be talked about for years after you get home. Some places in these chapters will fascinate everybody: Who can resist the view of Paris from the Eiffel Tower, after all? Others are for more specialized interests, like dolls, magic, or history.

Everyone should read these chapters and decide what parts of Paris they most want to see, so when you plan your itinerary later, every member of the family has plenty to look forward to. There is something in Paris for everyone, and this section will help everybody sort through the possibilities and find their own memorable spots. Welcome to Paris!

9. So Much to See, So Little Time

There's a difference between careful planning and being relentlessly left-brained. Travelers who expect to take a family hundreds or thousands of miles to a place nobody in the group has ever visited, whose culture nobody is familiar with, and perhaps whose language nobody speaks—well, those travelers really ought to do *some* planning.

On the other hand, *overplanning* can take the spontaneity, the flexibility, the *joy* out of a trip. The idea is to have fun, not to keep to a schedule. The ideal approach is usually to arrive at your destination with a very *short* list of must-see items, and a longer one of things you'd *like* to do but could live without. Leave your compulsions at home.

That said, I have to admit something: This is one of the hardest parts of travel for me. When I spend a lot of time and money to go somewhere neat, I feel like I have to see everything, do everything, in order to make my investment worthwhile. It takes a conscious effort for me to slow myself down and remember that it's not the *trip* I'm investing in... it's the *people*. I get better at it each year.

Chapters 10 to 17 are intended to make your family's planning easier. The top family attractions in Paris are here, as well as some more specialized places that might appeal to some members of your group. There's more than enough for one vacation here—much more. No matter how hard you try, you can't possibly go everywhere and see everything. It's much more fun not to try.

Everybody in the family should read these chapters and talk about them before you go on to the Planning Pages in Part III. For a trip like this, nothing is more important than for *everyone* to be in on the planning. This basic idea will do more to ensure a smooth and pleasant trip than the most carefully planned trip possible done by Mom and Dad alone. If it's a *family* trip, the *family* must plan it.

Three Rules of Family Travel

Every family is different, but there are some universal rules that will do more to guarantee a smooth trip than all the planning and all the money in the world. And they're so simple that they're easy to overlook. At the peril of your sanity... *don't!*

1. Everybody Gets His or Her First Choice

By the time they've read and talked about the next eight chapters, everyone will have learned about something they'd really like to see or do. Let them. If little sister wants to see the Doll Museum (Musée Poupée) more than anything else in Paris, big brother will make *no* complaints. In return, everyone will be tolerant of his desire to find Napoleon's sword and famous hat at the Army Museum (Musée de la Armée). This applies to parents, too. Everyone gets his or her first choice, and nobody complains about what anyone else chooses. Fact of the matter is, if everyone keeps an open mind, they might find themselves surprised many times a day. Everybody can appreciate the craftsmanship and intricacy of many antique dolls and models, and the Army Museum contains mysteries galore. The most important thing you can bring on a trip like this is a sense of excitement, a willingness to be surprised.

2. Plan Free Time

If you want to take a holiday where everybody's cranky and complaining, the best way to do it is to plan every minute of every day, to squeeze in an extra museum whenever possible, and to make sure you're on the go all the time. Forced marches are for armies on the move. A family on vacation needs a chance to breathe. Schedule free time. Spend an afternoon in the park, just sitting under a tree talking about what you've seen, reading a book, or people watching. Give yourself extra points for bringing along a picnic lunch.

You might think, "But we can go on a picnic at home! Why should we use our precious time in Paris for something like that?"

Short answer: Because you'll be sorry if you don't.

Longer answer: Everybody needs time to process and assimilate all the new and unusual things they've been exposed to, and because everyone is probably being more active than usual, their

Every visitor wants to see the arc

bodies need time to rest and recover. If bodies are tired, minds will soon follow. So plan a half day of relaxation a couple of times a week—a picnic, a leisurely cruise down the canal, a morning for everyone to sleep late and relax until after lunch.

Don't make every evening an extension of the day's sightseeing, either. Sometimes it's best just to stay in your apartment and watch TV, play a family game, or write in your journal. Keeping everybody rested and relaxed is a lot more essential to the success of a vacation than working in that extra museum.

3. Keep Your Eating and Sleeping on Schedule

When there's so much to do, so many new things to see, so much excitement, it's hard to slow down enough to stick to a routine. Kids are happiest when there's some structure to their lives, though, and that's true with older people as well. Unless your children are very small, you probably *should* stay out late one night, taking a cruise down the Seine to see the beauty of Paris at night, or going to the top of the Eiffel Tower after dark for a breathtaking panorama of the city. But don't do things like that every night. All members of the family will be better off sticking pretty close to their regular bedtimes. You'll all have more energy during the day if you get enough sleep at night, and that does wonders for everybody's disposition.

Eat your meals on a regular schedule, too. If you've been having lunch at 1 o'clock, don't start on a new museum at 12:30. Eat before you start and stop for a snack afterwards. Remember, too, the advice in Chapter 5 about emergency food: Never leave your apartment without a few granola bars or similar filling snack.

These three tips are the best insurance you can have against crabbiness. You might still be walking down a Paris street and hear the plaintive whines of "I'm hungry. I'm thirsty. I'm tired." But chances are it'll be from somebody else's kids.

Vary Your Activities

To get the most out of every place you go, plan contrasts. About the only thing that can diminish the grandeur of the Louvre is to see the Orsay on the same day. If you visit four churches in one day, chances are you won't remember any of them very well, even if one of them was Notre Dame. Seeing Paris from atop the Eiffel Tour will take away from the wonderful view you get from the Arc de Triomphe. Give everywhere you go its best chance to impress you: you're not there to compare—you're there to enjoy!

You can get an idea of how to do this sort of planning by taking a look at the itineraries in Chapter 19. If you spend the morning in a museum, spend the afternoon outdoors, perhaps exploring the quais along the Seine or searching out old twisting streets in the Marais. If you spend the morning in the Tuileries, save the Luxembourg Gardens for another day.

Tip: Follow the 2-Hour Rule. Never spend more than two hours in any museum, no matter how good it is, unless everyone agrees unhesitatingly. Hard floors make legs tired and attention wane. If a museum is too large to see in two hours, it's too large for three. Come back another day, if there's time. If the kids are pre-teen, 90 minutes is probably enough.

Sometimes that means you have to make tradeoffs. If you're spending just a week in Paris, you might not be able to see both the Louvre and the Orsay. It's hard to be ruthless, but you must. Save one for your next trip—it's nice to have something to look forward to next time.

Splitting Up

You may be taking a family holiday, but that doesn't mean you have to spend every waking moment in each other's company. After a couple of days in Paris, it's OK to split up sometimes. Everyone might have a better time if Dad and one kid go to the

Catacombs while Mom and the other two go to the zoo. It's even possible (in fact, I recommend it) to let the kids go off by themselves sometimes. That's mighty difficult for Mom and Dad. But once you've been in Paris for a few days, everyone is well oriented and can use the map, and everybody feels comfortable on the Metro, the older kids will appreciate an afternoon or two on their own.

How old should they be? Well, you know your own kids best, but 15- or 16-year-olds should be able to handle it just fine. Paris is very safe, there are Metro stations everywhere, and as long as they know where the apartment or hotel is, have some money, and know how to use the Metro, there's no reason why they shouldn't get along

Using Chapters 10-17

The next eight chapters contain the highlights of Paris, enough to keep a family busy for several trips. There are thousands more things to see and do in this wonderful place, but these are attractions and activities that have appealed to generations of local and visiting families alike.

All the information was accurate when Paris for Families *went to press, but unfortunately no one in Paris is likely to seek my approval before making changes. And things will change. Guaranteed. That's why entries don't list exact prices or opening hours: I've found at least some published information incorrect on every trip I've taken. Where there have been major changes, I'll post updates on the website for this book. The address is* http://www.interlinkbooks.com/ parisforfamilies.html *On that page is also a link for you to e-mail the author with corrections you discover on your trip.*

Attractions in the following chapters are generally listed like this: **Musée National du Moyen Age** *(The Musée Cluny) [6 Place Paul-Painlevé, 5th; Metro 10: Cluny-La Sorbonne; RER B: St-Michel. Closed Tuesday. Carte Musées. Under 18 free.]*

In the brackets after the name of the museum, or at the end on a lengthy entry, you'll find the address and arrondissement. (6 Place Paul-Painlevé, 5th). Next comes the nearest Metro line number and station (Metro 10: Cluny-La Sorbonne), and, if there's one quite close, the nearest RER line and station (RER B: St-Michel).

Opening hours are not listed because these

perfectly well. They'll probably find something their parents would never have seen, and may have the pleasure of leading everyone else to it later.

Even if they don't speak French, it's easy for them to get into a taxi and hand the driver a paper with the address of your apartment printed clearly on it. That's a perfect last resort for the nervous or hopelessly lost.

Carte Musées et Monuments

The Paris museum organization *Association interMusées* offers a special museum pass that may or may not be

are too often subject to change. In the summer you'll often find places open from 9 am until quite late, but perhaps only from 1 to 4:30 pm in the winter—and the shorter hours might run only from January to March, or might be from November until April. There's no way to keep up with it. It is very common, however, for museums to be closed one day per week, usually Monday or Tuesday, and this seldom changes. Where that is the case, it's given in the entry. If no closing day is listed, the attraction is open seven days a week.

If the entry lists Carte Musées, entry is free with the Carte Musées et Monuments, which is explained in this chapter. If there is no admission charge, the attraction is marked Free. Many places that do charge admission allow students below a specified age in free. That information is also given. Otherwise admission prices are not given— they change faster than Interlink's presses can keep up with them. Figure 35F as a reasonable average for an adult, but even when kids don't get in free, there might be a reduced price for them, so look for a sign that says Tarif reduit.

a good deal. You can buy a 1-day, 3-day, or 5-day pass, good on consecutive days at about 50 Paris museums, including some of the most popular, like the Louvre and the towers of Notre Dame, plus more than 20 additional attractions in the surrounding area. What's more, not only do pass-holders get in free, they can move directly to the front of the line, something that can be a real advantage at a place like the Louvre, where on a summer weekend the wait can be more than an hour just to buy a ticket.

Prices can be pretty good if you visit a lot of museums. A 1-day pass on my last trip cost 80F, probably enough to save me money if I went to three museums that day. A 3-day pass was 160F, so my pace of museum hopping could slow slightly. It would probably take only two museums a day to save money. A 5-day pass was 240F, even better value for the museum-minded traveler.

But—there's always a "but," isn't there?—even if you're a dedicated museum-goer, you might not want to buy passes. Most museums give free admission to anyone under a certain age—usually 12 or 18—and charge a reduced rate for students 18 to 25. And even if Mom and Dad buy a pass and plan on the kids getting in free, the kids will have to stand in the ticket line; the parents' passes won't let their kids bypass the line.

Before you buy a Carte Musée, make sure you know whether the attractions you want to see accept the pass. The Eiffel Tower, for example, does not. Also decide whether you'll be able to get to enough of the places on your list to make a pass worthwhile without running yourselves into the ground. Remember, the pace of a vacation needs to consider the person who tires most easily. That might be the 6-year-old. But it might also be Dad!

Recommendations

✔ Make sure everybody gets his or her first choice of what to see.

✔ Build free time into your schedule. People need rest even from a vacation.

✔ Don't spend more than two hours on any one thing unless everybody clamors for more.

✔ Check the *Paris for Families* web page for updated information.

✔ Don't be compulsive. You can't see everything anyway, so just have fun.

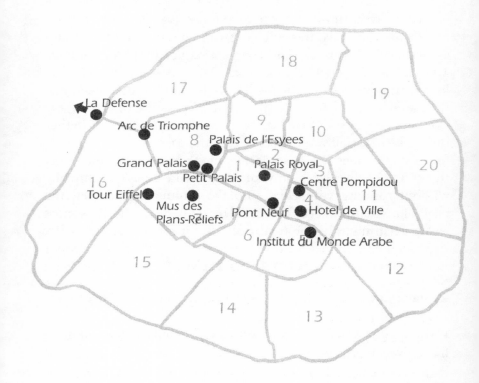

La Defense

Arc de Triomphe

Palais de l'Esyees

8

Grand Palais

Petit Palais

1

Palais Royal

Centre Pompidou

3

Tour Eiffel

Mus des
Plans-Reliefs

Pont Neuf

Hotel de Ville

4

Institut du Monde Arabe

6

17

18

19

9

10

2

16

20

11

7

15

12

14

13

Chapter 10 Highlights

10. Marvelous Structures

There are a handful of architectural landmarks that everyone recognizes, buildings that are part of our shared human heritage. London has its Big Ben tower, New York its Empire State Building. Everyone recognizes Egypt's pyramids and knows that the fanciful turrets and spires of St. Basil's are in Moscow (even if they can't remember the name of the church). A Paris landmark? You don't even have to think about it.

The Eiffel Tower.

Rumor has it that in 1958 a tourist tried to leave Paris without seeing the Eiffel Tower and he was taken from the airport in chains and placed in a cell at the top. Probably an exaggeration. Actually, it would be nearly impossible to *avoid* seeing the Tower. It's visible from almost everywhere west of the Marais.

The Eiffel Tower—*Tour Eiffel*—is only one of the eye-popping structures that create wonderful memories... and incredible photographs... of Paris. In this chapter we can wander around the city looking for that eye candy. Let's start at the top.

Tour Eiffel

When the Eiffel Tower was built for an exhibition in 1889, Parisians hated it, called it an eyesore, and were glad it was only temporary and would be torn down after the festivities. Well, a lot of Parisians have come and gone, and the Tower is still there. The Parisians? They would rather give up snails and red wine than the Eiffel Tower. OK—not the wine.

It takes patience to actually go up in the Tower; lines are very long, especially in the summer, and a wait of two hours is not

Two Bridges

While the Left Bank, the Right Bank, and the Islands have very different feels to them, they are extremely easy to move between. In central Paris, the Seine is crossed by some three dozen bridges (ponts) of all sorts. You'll find pedestrian bridges, motorway bridges, bridges that connect islands to the mainland or islands to each other. Some are very old; some are brand new. There are two bridges, though, that everybody pays attention to.

The **Pont Neuf** translates as "New Bridge." Well, it was new in 1578. Now it's the oldest bridge in Paris. In the beginning it was lined with stalls and tents of all sorts of merchants, but, unusually for the times, no permanent houses. Few bridges, probably, have appeared in more paintings. The bridge connects the area of the Louvre and Châtelet-Les Halles on the Right Bank with the St-Germain area on the Left, cutting across the tip of the Ile de la Cité.

Pont Alexandre III is the most ornate bridge in the city. Built for the same world's fair that produced the Grand and Petit Palais—and situated right next to them—the bridge is covered with fanciful sculptures and gilt statuary. On a sunny day the view (and a photo) from the Left Bank of the ornate bridge and ornate buildings is indeed marvelous. The bridge joins the Grand Palais and Petit Palais on the Right Bank with Invalides on the Left.

The Pont Neuf is the oldest bridge in Paris. La Samaritaine is in the Right Bank end of the bridge

uncommon. That's OK. The kids will insist on going up and they're right. You're here to do touristy things, after all. You can take turns standing in the line while everyone else wanders around gawking at the river, pondering the bust of Gustave Eiffel (the engineer who built it), munching at the food kiosks, or relaxing in the nearby park.

You'll want to decide in advance how high you want to go, because each level (*étage*) has a different price. The first level, 57 meters (187 feet), costs less than 25F. You can mail your postcards from the post office there, or watch a video presentation on the history of the Tower. The neat double-decker elevators zip you up in seconds or you can climb the 360 steps to the platform.

If your ticket is for the second level—about 45F—you can stay on the elevator or climb 340 more steps (700 so far) for a fabulous view from 115m (377 feet). The **Jules Verne Restaurant** is on this level, but it might not be the place to take the whole family for dinner unless you've booked well in advance and have a credit card with a high melt-down level—it's very expensive.

The Pont Alexandre III near the Grand Palais, is often called the most beautiful bridge in Paris

But what's the point, really, if you don't go all the way to the top? That ticket is more than 60F but the view is breathtaking. Now you're 275m (about 900 feet) high and, if it's a very clear day, you can see for more than 40 miles. The Tower is bigger than most people expect: Even the smallest platform—the third level—holds 800 people. And very few of them have walked up! To do that you'd have to climb 1,652 steps. Even walking down, which people sometimes do, is exhausting.

For a real treat, go twice—once during the day for the most detailed view, and once late at night for a spectacular panorama over the City of Light. The Tower is open until midnight in the summer and until 11 PM in the winter, and after 8 or 9 o'clock the lines are much shorter. (In fact, my first trip up the Eiffel Tower was late on a warm summer night in the rain—very romantic. But that's another book.) *[Champ de Mars, 7ᵗʰ; Metro 6: Bir Hakeim; RER C: Champ de Mars.]*

Arch Rivals

Triumphal arches are scattered all over the globe, but none is more famous than the second great Paris landmark, the **Arc de Triomphe** *[Place Charles de Gaulle, 8ᵗʰ; Metro 1, 2, 6; RER A: Charles de Gaulle-Etoile. Carte Musées. Open until 11 p.m. Tues. through Sat; until 6:30 Sun. and Mon. Under 12 free.]*. This great monument to Napoleon's conquests (but not finished until fifteen years after his death) sits in the middle of a conjunction of twelve roads—*Etoile* (star)—at the

Not everything is as grand as the Arc de Triomphe

end of the Champs Élysées. The swarm of traffic buzzing around the arch is an amazing sight in itself. It's no place for the timid! The street has no lane markings and cars appear to just wander wherever they choose—at high speed. It's a driver's worst nightmare.

You will want to go out to the arch, but please: *Do not try to cross on the surface!* Use the pedestrian underpass from the avenues Champs Élysées or Grande Armée.

Beneath the arch is the Tomb of the Unknown Soldier with its eternal flame. The relief sculptures on the sides of the arch are vivid depictions of Napoleon's victories and other French triumphs. But don't miss the view from the top. You can take the elevator, but if it's not working (usually my fate) it's at least more walkable than the Eiffel Tower. The total climb is 273 steps (a place to rest at No. 124) with toilets 169 steps up. At just 46 steps from the top there's a large hall with lots of places to sit down, a gift shop, and pictures of the arch over the years—but nothing to drink, so bring your water bottle. They could probably make up the French national budget by selling Cokes here for 100F.

The view from the top (50m or 165 feet) is terrific. The Eiffel Tower is nearby, you can see the sun glinting off the white façade of Sacré-Coeur, you get a nice look at Montmartre, a great view up the Champs Élysées, and a good look at la Grande Arche at La Défense.

Like New York's Wall Street and London's City, Paris's La Défense is a business city within the city. But because it was planned as a unit, it has a modernist architectural flair that's unique. While this is more a place for corporate suits that tourist shorts, there's enough to do to make a trip worth considering. There's a large Imax theater, an automobile museum, and plenty of shopping, but the thing that draws the crowds is **La Grande Arche** *[La Défense; Metro 1; RER A: La Défense.]*

The arch, a hollow concrete cube, is more than twice as tall as the Arc de Triomphe— 106m (348 feet) and large enough to contain Notre Dame Cathedral. Access to the top is, blessedly, via elevator! The view from the top is superb, but you are rather far out here, and central Paris landmarks are less spectacular seen from here.

Four Palaces

If you're looking for wonderful buildings to gawk at, here are three within a short walk of each other. You'll probably

> *Tip:* About halfway down the Rue du Faubourg-St-Honoré you will come to the Rue Royale. Turn left here and walk to the building that looks like a Greek temple. This is the church of St. Mary Magdalene, known as "La Madeleine." The building was planned as a church, then a military memorial, then a church again, then a railway terminal, and finally a church. There's a market on the east side, and the food store Fauchon, the finest in Paris—and that's saying a lot. The view from the portico of La Madeleine is gorgeous, down the Rue Royale, through the Place de la Concorde, and across the Seine to the Assemblée Nationale, a notable building in its own right. Originally built as a home for the Duchesse de Bourbon (daughter of Louis XIV) it is now the meeting-place of the French parliament.

see them as you walk around Paris, whether you're looking for them or not.

The **Grand Palais** *[Avenue Eisenhower, 8th; Metro 1, 13: Champs Élysées-Clemenceau]* was built for the Paris World's Fair of 1900 and now houses important temporary exhibitions, as well as the Palais de la Découverte (Chapter 15) in the west wing. As you stroll along the Champs Élysées or along the Seine, you'll enjoy the Art-Nouveau style of this building and its smaller sister across the street, the **Petit Palais** *[Avenue Winston Churchill, 8th; Metro 1,13: Champs Élysées-Clemenceau. Closed Monday]* that houses the Musée de Beaux-Arts.

If you cross the Champs Élysées in front of the Grand Palais and walk a block up Avenue de Marigny, you'll come to the **Palais de l'Élysée**, official residence of the president of France. It's not open to the public but you can take a photograph of the outside and the

Standing guard in front of the Palais Elysées, the presidential mansion

smartly uniformed guards. *[55 Rue du Faubourg-St-Honoré, 8th; Metro 1, 13: Champs Élysées Clemenceau]*

A walk past the president's house along the Rue du Faubourg-St-Honoré will take you past the British embassy and a selection of interesting shops and churches, and will end at the broad plaza, Place André-Malraux. Across the plaza is the Comédie Française, France's national theater, and behind it the **Palais Royal** *[Place du Palais-Royal, 1st; Metro 1, 7: Palais Royal-Louvre].* The buildings are now occupied by government offices and are not open to the public. But the colonnaded gardens are delightful (despite the jarring presence of countless stumplike sculptures).

The palace was built by Cardinal Richelieu, the prime minister, in the 1630s, and he left it to King Louis XIII. A succession of royalty lived here off and on until the revolution, when the place deteriorated badly and the area became notorious for gambling, prostitution, and thievery. There are no such problems today. The gardens are lovely and worth a stop if you're in the area.

Other Notable Buildings

Do make time to walk past the **Center Georges-Pompidou** *[Place Georges- Pompidou, 4th; Metro 11: Rambuteau. Closed Tuesday. Carte Musées. Under 16 free]* This is what you'd look like if you sneezed hard enough to turn yourself inside out. Ventilation pipes, plumbing, electrical conduits, stairways, elevators are hanging everywhere, and all are painted in bright primary colors (blue for air conditioning, green for water, yellow for electricity, and red for human access). Guards grow weary of explaining that, yes, it is indeed finished. The building may look like an alien spacecraft, but it houses France's national collection of twentieth-century art, the Musée d'Art Moderne (Chapter 13), which is more than enough reason to visit.

Another striking, if less garish, modern building is the **Institut du Monde Arabe** *[1 Rue des Fossés-St-Bernard, 5th; Metro 10: Cardinal Lemoine. Closed Monday. Carte Musées. Under 12 free]* This is a joint venture of twenty Arab countries to increase understanding of Islamic culture. Mechanical light screens and shutters control the light entering the building and are both works of art and masterpieces of engineering at once, a rare combination. The seventh-floor museum displays art representing the wide variety of Arab culture.

On the Right Bank across from the Ile de la Cité is the Paris city hall, the **Hôtel de Ville** *[Place Hôtel de Ville, 4th; Metro 1, 11: Hôtel de Ville].* The building is not open to the public, except for rare art exhibitions, but it's a good spot to catch sight of visiting dignitaries, who are usually welcomed here. A guillotine was set up here during the Revolution, and the original building was burned to the ground during the uprisings of 1871, although the new one is a good copy. The broad plaza is popular for impromptu soccer matches in the summertime, but there's fun for everybody in the winter: The plaza is flooded and frozen, and everybody in Paris, it seems, comes here to ice skate.

There's a carnival atmosphere then with food kiosks and carousels—including one double-decker. If your visit is in the winter, make it a point to stop. Skates can be rented by the hour.

Marvelous structures don't have to be huge like the Eiffel Tower or eye-catching like the Pompidou Center. Some of the neatest are quite small, but maybe a highlight of the trip if you have a model maker in the family. If you visit the Army Museum at Invalides (Chapter 15), make a short stop at the **Musée des Plans-Reliefs** (relief maps) *[Hôtel National des Invalides, 6 Blvd des Invalides , 7*[th]*; Metro 8, La Tour Maubourg or 13, Varenne; RER C: Invalides. Closed Monday. Carte Musées. Under 12 free.]* The museum displays models of 24 fortified cities made in the late seventeenth century for Louis XIV as an aid to planning military strategy. The cities, which are immensely detailed, are built on a scale of 1:600, and provide an authentic view of what seventeenth-century cities looked like. The museum is on the fourth floor of the East wing of the Army Museum.

The ornate Hôtel de Ville is the Paris city hall

Recommendations

✔ If you have time, visit the Eiffel Tower both by day and by night. The views, both of and from the Tower, are very different.

✔ Climb things—or at least take the elevator—whenever possible. Paris is a city of unrivaled views.

✔ Paris has many marvelous structures. As you walk, pay attention to the details of buildings you pass: roofs, doorways, windows, and courtyards. You'll be fascinated.

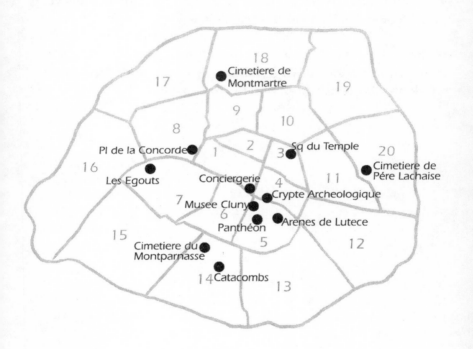

Chapter 11 Highlights

11. Graves, Ghosts, and Ruins

Everybody likes to be scared, at least a little, as long as they know they're really safe. Kids in giant roller coasters plummet down narrow tracks faster than their screams can overtake them. Horror movies play to theaters packed with kids of all ages and of both sexes. So let's spend a chapter in some of the creepiest places in Paris, places that are a cinch to be among the most talked-about stops on your trip. We'll start in a place that's guaranteed to make the hair on the back of your neck stand up straight.

The Terrifying Trio

The Catacombs

Descend 120 circular steps down, down into the dim underworld of Paris. You've entered the city's most unusual attraction.

When you reach the bottom at last, signs will point you down a narrow series of tunnels. For ten minutes or so (it seems like an hour) you'll thread your way through narrow passages little more than 2 meters high (about 7 feet) and a bit more than a meter wide (4 feet). The walls are close and damp;

Tip: *The Catacombs are open just two hours at a time, usually Tuesday through Friday 2-4 pm and Saturday and Sunday 9-11 am and 2-4 pm. Get there a minimum of 30 minutes early. Even in winter a line of 250 people by opening time is not uncommon.*

dark side passages suggest unseen terrors. Although there are enough electric lights for you to find your way easily, the place feels like it should be lit by torches. This is no place for claustrophobes.

Suddenly there's a change in the limestone walls—they're not stone any more: The walls looming over you are made of stacks

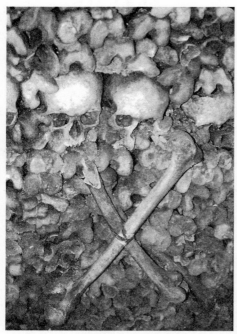

of human bones and skulls! As far away as you can see, there's nothing but bones—artfully arranged here, scattered and broken there—countless millions of bones! For the next fifteen minutes you wander along subterranean passageways, through underground courtyards and plazas, past altars made of stone and bone. At first the effect is chilling; after awhile you get used to it and the feeling is more of amazement: How many bones are there? How did they get here? How old are they?

The Catacombs are the creepiest attraction of Paris

About 1785, Paris began to close many of its cemeteries and move the bones of at least 2 million people (some say up to 6 million) to provide more building space. Remains were moved churchyard by churchyard, and stacked in old stone quarries beneath the city. Signs in the tunnels identify the churchyard each section of remains came from and the date it was moved. Some of these bones are of Parisians of more than a thousand years ago.

In spite of the undoubtedly creepy feel to the whole place, don't be alarmed. While there are more than 50 miles (90 km) of tunnels down here, you can't get lost; now the side passages are barred with ancient iron gates. There's plenty of light, but if it's convenient, bring along a flashlight for looking into odd corners and down closed-off passageways. During World War II, the French Resistance forces made their headquarters down here—perfect for an "underground" movement! The Nazis never found them.

At the end of the route you'll climb about 80 steps to the exit, but before you emerge into the sunlight again, an attendant will ask to inspect the bags and backpacks of everyone in your group, just to make sure you haven't tried to spirit away a bone or two.

When you come out, you'll find yourself on Rue Rémy Dumoncel, a fair distance from the entrance. To get back to your starting point, turn right, then right again on Avenue du General Leclerc. A 10- to 15-minute walk takes you back to Place Denfert-Rochereau. [1 Place Denfert-Rochereau, 14th; Metro 4, 6; RER B: Denfert-Rochereau. Closed Monday.]

The Conciergerie

The River Seine is lined with distinctive and historic buildings; none is more so than the Conciergerie. In many ways, this is the Paris equivalent of the Tower of London—palace, prison, military garrison. Its past is a chilling one.

A Grave Matter

If it sounds a bit creepy to think of cemeteries as tourist attractions, think again. In nice weather, the graveyards of Paris are popular with visitors from all over the world who like to take in a bit of sun and see the tombs of the famous and influential. Here are the three most popular.

Thousands of people a year flock to the Cimetiére du Pére Lachaise [16 Rue du Repos, 20th; Metro 2, 3: Pére Lachaise. Free.], the most famous cemetery in Paris. Look for the last resting places of rock star Jim Morrison, composer Frederic Chopin, playwright Oscar Wilde, singer Edith Piaf, novelist Marcel Proust, dancer Isadora Duncan, and actress Sarah Bernhardt. (Actually, not all of Chopin, who was Polish, is here—his heart is in Warsaw.)

An even more artistic spot might be the Cimetiére de Montmartre [20 Avenue Rachel, 18th; Metro 2, 13: Place de Clichy. Free.] Here you can pay your respects to composers Jacques Offenbach and Hector Berlioz, writers Alexandre Dumas and Heinrich Heine, painter Edgar Degas, dancer Nijinsky, and many others.

A third cemetery worth a visit for those so inclined is the Cimetiére du Montparnasse [3 Blvd. Edgar Quinet, 14th; Metro 6: Edgar Quinet. Free.] This is the place to commune with the spirits of writers-philosophers Jean-Paul Sartre and Simone de Beauvoir, the composers Saint-Saëns and Franck, the novelist Guy de Maupassant and a host of others.

The Conciergerie was built beginning about 1310 by King Philip the Fair, and the next several kings lived there. By 1370, though, the king had moved elsewhere and the building was used for quartering troops, for judicial offices, and for housing prisoners, a function it served for more than 500 years. The most notorious time for the Conciergerie, though, was during the French Revolution of 1789, when it was known as the "anteroom of the guillotine." Prisoners, including the Queen Marie-Antoinette, were held here awaiting their executions. A list of the more than 2,700 people who spent their last nights here during that time is displayed on the second floor.

You can walk through much of the fortress now. Most impressive is

The Conciergerie has stood beside the Seine for 800 years

the vast **Hall of Men-at-Arms**. This dark room with its vaulted ceilings and tall columns was a gathering place for soldiers, a dining room for officials, a court of justice, and a place for royal banquets with up to 2,000 guests at a time. Visit the reconstruction of the cell where Marie-Antoinette spent her last days, and the tiny dank cells where prisoners of lesser stature were packed.

The towers along the river have histories of their own, too. The square one—the one on the east end—is the **Clock Tower**, the newest of the towers, built in 1350 to house the first public clock in France. The clock you see now replaced the original in 1585. Next are the three round towers. First is the **Roman Tower**, commemorating the Roman ruins that lie under many of the buildings here. Next is the **Silver Tower**, once the stronghold where the royal treasury was kept. The westernmost tower is the most grisly. This is the dreaded **Bonbec Tower**, site of the torture chamber. From its windows all Paris could once

Luckily they don't use the old prison anymore

listen to the "interrogation" of state prisoners.

If you want to walk through ancient rooms where the presence of ghosts feels almost palpable, don't miss the Conciergerie. Most signs and exhibits are in French but videos have English subtitles. *[1 quai de l'Horloge, 1ˢᵗ; Metro 4: Cité. Under 12 free.]*

Arènes de Lutèce

Next is a place that doesn't seem terrifying at all, the Arènes de Lutèce, a Roman theater almost 2,000 years old, named for the Roman city Lutetia that became the Paris we know today. Sitting in the middle of a park in the Latin Quarter just east of Rue Monge, the Arènes de Lutèce is now just a quiet place for passersby to relax on the ancient stone seats and eat their lunches. On the floor of the arena you'll probably see young boys playing soccer or old men playing boules. But if you could step back to around the year A.D. 250, you would see a very different sight.

Perhaps there might be a play or a circus. But not all the entertainment was so benign. The arena also housed gladiatorial combat, and you might arrive in time to watch two men trying to hack each other to death while 15,000 screaming spectators urged them on. You might arrive on a day when wild animals and men were pitted against each other in this very amphitheater.

Now, as you walk across this dusty arena, your eyes can look up on the same tiers of stone seats that were the last things many warrior eyes ever saw. Those chambers behind the iron

Instead of gladiators and wild beasts, young soccer players now use the
Arlènes de Lutèce

grates: Can we picture lions in there?

If there are ghosts anywhere, there must be some around the Arènes de Lutèce. If you have an imagination and any sort of interest in history, this is a place that ought to put them both into overdrive. Because the arena just sits in the middle of the park, it's always free and open to the public during the daylight hours. [*Rue de Navarre, 5th; Metro 7: Place Monge, 10: Jussieu. Free.*]

The French Underground

What shall we call this section—the low point of your vacation? A tour that will take your breath away? The mind reels at the possible puns and double entendres. Let's go into the dark realm, the country that was stalked by the Phantom of the Opera, the passages that were home to the wicked Thénadier who haunted Paris through Les Misèrables, stripping the dead of their possessions, cutting off their fingers for their rings, and even pulling the teeth of the wounded living for their gold fillings. These are the sewers of Paris, **Les Egouts**. The tour is one of the most popular in Paris, especially among the young.

Actually the tour of the Paris sewers is anything but dark and scary, nothing at all like the Catacombs. The sewer system is a complete city beneath the city and it's possible to traverse all of Paris beneath its streets. In fact, you'll find the same street signs below ground that you will above, making it possible to find your way as you wander the 2100km (1300 miles) of sewers, maybe emerging from one of the 26,000 manholes!

Tourists actually have access to only a kilometer or so of the vast network; no one will let you wander away. But along the way you'll be treated (if that's the right word) to a barrage of information about the history, construction, and workings of this wonder of the world, seeing more than you imagined about automatic sewer flushing machines, underground train networks, and waste processing. You'll emerge (perhaps gratefully) with a new appreciation for one of the many unseen things that make modern civilization possible, and with a sightseeing story your friends back home just won't believe!

It's a very well done tour with multimedia presentations and signs and information in French, English, German, and Spanish. And yes, there's a gift shop. Imagine the possibilities! The entrance is on the Left Bank end of the Pont de l'Alma. *[93 Quai d'Orsay, 7ᵗʰ; Metro 9: Alma-Marceau (across the bridge); RER C: Pont de l'Alma. Closed Thursday and Friday. Carte Musées. Under 5 free.]*

The Tombs of Heroes

Around 1760, King Louis XV decided to build a grand church to house the relics of St. Geneviève. The glorious building that rose from his plan was used for both religious and secular purposes over the next century, but finally became one of the best-known civic monuments in France, the **Panthéon** *[Place du Panthéon, 5ᵗʰ;*

Metro 10: Cardinal Lemoine; RER B: Luxembourg. Carte Musées. Under 12 free]. This is the last resting place of the greats of France: Voltaire, Rousseau, Curie, Hugo, Zola, and others. The dome, where Foucault hung his famous pendulum, is the most spectacular in Paris. The crypt, down 40 winding stone steps, is cool and silent. Foot-steps echo and whispers carry throughout the space. In the hot summer the Panthéon is an oasis of cool and quiet; in winter, security guards in heavy coats huddle around

The Pantheon, tomb of the greatest French heroes

a few heaters. There's a large cutaway model of the building at the back left that shows how the edifice was built. Even if you don't go in, there's a great view of the Eiffel Tower from the portico. Information is available here in several languages besides French.

A Trip Ending in Ruins

Because Paris is nearly two millennia old, you can find a lot of really old stuff. One of the best places to look is the **Crypte Archéologique** *[Place du Parvis, 4th; Metro 4: Cité. Carte Musées. Under 12 free.]*, beneath the plaza in front the Notre Dame Cathedral. The Ile de la Cité was once lower than it is today. As new buildings were built atop the rubble of older ones, the walls and foundations of the first structures on the island became covered over and finally forgotten. Bits and pieces of the original cities of the Parisii and Romans would occasionally turn up as buildings were built—or destroyed—but it wasn't until excavations in 1965 that a serious effort was made to study and understand them.

Now visitors can view artifacts, wall fragments, cellars, sewers, and foundations from almost 2,100 years ago up through the nineteenth century. Exhibits are well presented and accompanied by good descriptions in both French and English. Antiquarians of all ages will be fascinated by a half-hour in the crypt.

No one with an interest in medieval times should miss the **Musée National du Moyen Age** (The Musée Cluny) *[6 Place*

The entrance to the Cluny Museum looks like the monastery it once was

Paul-Painlevé, 5th; Metro 10: Cluny-La Sorbonne; RER B: St-Michel. Closed Tuesday. Carte Musées. Under 18 free.], a 500-year-old building that was once the home of the Abbot of Cluny. Highlights include the famous tapestries "The Lady and the Unicorn" but some people might find the story behind the sculptures in Gallery 8 interesting. During the French Revolution that resulted in King Louis XVI losing his head in an encounter with a guillotine, the mob, intent on destroying all things royal, sacked Notre

Dame Cathedral and pulled down the statues of kings that lined the walls of the church. Believing them to be statues of French kings, the mob cut off their heads, too. Stupid mob. The statues were of the Biblical kings of Judah. The heads were rediscovered in 1977.

You can also see plenty of Roman artifacts here, including old Roman baths. Children without an interest in the times might find the museum tedious, but others will enjoy the carved altars, icons from Eastern churches, countless religious artifacts, and the lovely small chapel with its wonderful vaulted ceiling. Museum pamphlets are available in many languages.

Sober Reminders

Paris has numerous reminders of sad and painful times, and you're bound to come across several on your wanderings. For example, at the tip of the park behind Notre Dame Cathedral (Square Jean XXIII), you'll find the **Mémorial de la Déportation,** a memorial to the 200,000 French who were deported to Nazi concentration camps. Not far away, just north of the river, is the **Mémorial du Martyr Juif Inconnu** *[17 Rue Geoffroy-l'Asnier, 4th]*, an eternal flame commemorating the Jews who died in the Holocaust. There is a Holocaust research library here, as well. The memorial is jarring in this area of picturesque old streets —perhaps just what was intended.

You can't go to Paris and not see the **Place de la Concorde**. It sits between the Tuileries and the Champs-Élysées and has a giant, 3000-year-old Egyptian obelisk in its center. You can't miss it. But that's all most visitors to Paris know about it, except the street is almost impossible to cross. It's a fantastic sight and no one associates it with anything gruesome, except with the possibility of some tourist being run over by a fleet of buses. But the obelisk sits of the site of the guillotine that in 1793–94 lopped off the heads of more than a thousand people, including Louis XVI

An ancient Egyptian obelisk stands in the Place de la Concorde

and Marie-Antoinette.

Unless you're staying in the neighborhood, you might not get to the **Square du Temple** *[Metro 3: Temple]*. This is just a cheerful park now with lots of trees and green space, plenty of room for running around, and a small children's playground. It wasn't always so. The monks, members of the militant religious order Knights Templar, once had a community here and were known for their willingness to give sanctuary to felons fleeing the wrath of the king. The area was soon filled with debtors and desperados. Eventually the king felt he'd been patient long enough, burned a number of the monks at the stake, and built a palace, a dungeon and a prison here. Ironically, Louis XVI was held here before his execution at Concorde. Napoleon tore the buildings down when he became emperor.

Any place as old and as large as Paris is going to have its share of old corners, unsavory tales, and scary traditions, exactly the sort of thing someone in your group will find to be the highlight of the trip. Enjoy your goosebumps!

Recommendations

✔ Unless the kids are small or your agenda is packed, consider the Catacombs. They're unique, and visitors soon get over the creepy feeling. Most kids think they're cool.

✔ Refresh your memory a little about the French Revolution before you visit Paris. You'll find connections to it everywhere you go.

✔ Talk about what it might have been like to live in earlier times: Roman Paris, medieval Paris, and revolutionary times. It helps make places come alive for kids and will help them make the same sorts of connections in school.

Tourists are rarely beheaded at the Place de la Concorde these days

Basilique St-Denis

18

Sacre-Coeur

17

19

9

10

8

2

St-Eustache

3

20

St-Germain l'Auxerrois

16

Saint-Chapelle

Eglise du Dome

11

7

Notre-Dame

St-Germain des Pres

6

5

15

Mosquee de Paris

12

14

13

Chapter 12 Highlights

12. Holy Ground

The French are certainly ambivalent when it comes to matters of religion. They've numbered a few saints among their kings, yet Parisians have cheerfully murdered each other over religious differences. When the Revolution came, some of the most beautiful churches were converted to secular use, and the new government began a program to pull them down. A decade or two later, churches were in vogue again.

In twenty-first-century Paris you'll find many churches, mostly Roman Catholic, but with all the world's major religions represented, and a substantial indifference to the formal practice of religion: only about 20 percent of the French attend religious services each week. Massacres no longer take place.

Certainly if you're a church-going family, you'll want to go to church in Paris; even if your command of the language is poor or non-existent, you'll feel a special devotion in being with others of your faith so far from home. You'll also have a good opportunity to meet ordinary Parisians on their home ground, away from the world of tourism.

If formal religion is not part of your family's normal life, you might still find yourself in church. There are several churches in Paris worth visiting for historical and aesthetic reasons.

Notre Dame Cathedral

Let's spend a little while in this, the most important church in Paris and one of the most famous in the world.

First look at the outside of the church, which is almost unchanged from 1330. The broad plaza was created in the nineteenth century when the church was almost completely hemmed in by other buildings. In the center of the square, you'll see a bronze plaque, the point from which all distances in France are measured. Stand at the plaque facing the church. The statue of the mounted horseman on your right is the Emperor Charlemagne. Actually, aside from reasons of Gallic pride, he doesn't really belong here. Paris wasn't his capital at all and he seldom visited the place, which he thought dirty and uncivilized.

Notre Dame is one of the great cathedrals of the world

Holy Ground

Behind you is the entrance to the **Crypte Archéologique** (Chapter 11) and in front of you is the cathedral where popes have prayed, where Joan of Arc was condemned, where Napoleon was crowned—or, more accurately, where he took the crown out of the Pope's hands and crowned himself. The towers of Notre Dame are almost 70 meters high (230 feet) and the church was the standard by which all medieval cathedrals were judged. The collection of statues on the front is called the **Gallery of Kings**, and represents the 28 kings of Judah. These are reproductions. Remember from Chapter 11 that the originals were mistaken for French kings during the Revolution and decapitated.

Entering the church from the main portal on the west end is like walking into an enormous cave, cool and dark. (In fact, the only complaint most visitors have about Notre Dame is that it's so dark that it's hard to see some of the dazzling artwork.) Visitors are steered into walking counterclockwise around the church but there's ample opportunity to veer aside. Photography is permitted, but difficult because it's so dark. (Please don't use flash, which is blinding in the dim light. Besides, the church is so vast—about 130 meters, or 425 feet—that your flash won't do much good. Use a fast film of ISO 1000 or 1600... or just buy postcards.)

Visitors cluster close to the high altar to get a good view of the famous rose windows. As you face the altar, the window on your left (north) focuses on the Old Testament, while the south window on your right features New Testament figures. Both windows are more than 700 years old, although the South window has required some restoration work.

Spend a little time wandering through the church admiring the 150 years of backbreaking human labor and devotion it took to build this place, and admiring the art that fills it. Frankly, the church is so filled with the buzz and shuffling of visitors, even during Mass, that it's difficult to capture the devotional feelings the church is supposed to inspire. If you'd like, though, there are

Quasimodo must be fit from climbing Notre Dame's towers all day

quiet side chapels you can slip into for a few minutes of private reflection.

It probably won't be long before the kids are ready for something more active. Good. Here's a chance to let them burn off some of their adolescent energy. Let them climb the 386 steep steps up the tower. Quasimodo, the bell-ringer who lived in the Tower and was the title character of Victor Hugo's *The Hunchback of Notre Dame*, must have had the strongest legs in Paris!

Once they make it to the top, the kids will have an extraordinary view of all Paris, plus a close-up of the famous gargoyles. Whether the parents will have the legs and wind to get that far is something only they know. Entrance to the Towers is on the north side of the church. *[Place du Parvis de Notre-Dame, 4ᵗʰ; Metro 4: Cité; RER B: St-Michel/Notre Dame. Church: Free; Towers: Carte Musées. Under 12 free.]*

Once everybody's back down on the ground, they might like to rest for a few minutes in the pretty **Square du Jean XXIII**, the formal gardens behind the cathedral. Here you'll get a picturesque view of the Seine, and a good view of the flying buttresses that made it possible for twelfth-century masons to build this church in the first place. Without these innovative supports, the building would have collapsed under its own weight long before it was finished.

If you want to know more and it's Wednesday, Saturday, or Sunday afternoon, you might visit the **Musée de Notre-Dame**, a small collection of exhibits and artifacts that go back to the building of the cathedral. The museum is across the street from the north side of the church. *[10 Rue Cloitre-Notre-Dame, 4ᵗʰ; Metro 4: Cité. Closed Mon., Tues., Thurs., Fri. Open 2-6 p.m.]*

A Symphony in Stained Glass

Visitors throng Notre Dame, and its size and variety of things to see and do probably make it the best church destination for families. But if I had time to return to only one Paris church, it would be nearby **Sainte-Chapelle**. It is part of the old royal palace of the Conciergerie, and was built in 1248 by King Louis IX as a royal chapel, and to house important relics, like Christ's crown of thorns (now at Notre Dame), which the king had purchased.

The lower chapel itself would be worth a visit, decorated in gold leaf and scarlet trim. This was where the king's servants worshiped. But nothing can prepare you for the sight that awaits

you after you climb the narrow staircase to the upper chapel, the one reserved for the king and royal family.

Your first thought is "How does it stay up? It's all glass!" Indeed, the fifteen vast stained-glass windows take up far more of the walls than brick and mortar do. Glass extends from a few feet above the floor clear to the magnificent arched

The flying buttresses that allow Notre Dame to stand

ceiling, with only narrow bands of stone holding them all together. The effect is dazzling. In fact, the windows were once even *larger*, going clear to the floor, before the lower quarter of each window was removed after the Revolution, when the chapel became a storehouse for legal documents. Stupid mob.

Nearly all the remaining glass is authentic thirteenth-century, though. The windows tell the history of the world and portray the French royal dynasty as a continuation of the Hebrew kings. The windows tell vivid stories from the Bible from Genesis through the Apocalypse. You can find cards in numerous languages at the rear of the chapel that explain the windows in detail. If you go, by all means, choose a sunny day, when the colors will be at their most brilliant. *[4 Boulevard du Palais, 4th; Metro 4: Cité. Carte Musées. Under 7 free.]*

Napoleon's Tomb

After Napoleon had been defeated at Waterloo after keeping all of Europe in an uproar for fifteen years, he was sent to exile on the

Dome Church at Invalides houses the tomb of Napoléon

remote island of St. Helena, where he died in 1821. So fearful of his popular influence were his enemies, however, that not even his ashes were allowed to return to Paris until almost twenty years had passed. Now his tomb in l'Église du Dôme (Dôme Church) is one of the most revered monuments in Paris.

The church, built between in 1677 and 1735, was once intended as a burial place for royalty, but with royalty out of favor by the end of the century, it became a place for displaying captured enemy battle flags and souvenirs, guarded by pensioned soldiers living in the adjacent military hospital Les Invalides.

To accommodate Napoleon's tomb, the crypt of the church was opened up and his coffin (or rather, his *six* coffins, one inside the other like Russian dolls) is visible from both the nave and the crypt. Dôme Church now also houses the tombs of other French military heroes as well as his brother Joseph Bonaparte, once the king of Spain. *[129 Rue de Grenelle, 7ᵗʰ; Metro 8, 13; RER C: Invalides. Carte Musées. Under 12 free.]*

> ***Tip:*** *The exit from the Metro and RER comes up in the middle of a lovely Esplanade that is a good place for everyone to run off a little steam. It's a popular spot for rollerblading, boules, Frisbee-tossing, and people-watching. The Metro is about halfway between the Seine and Dôme Church.*

Other Spiritual Places

You can see the spectacular white profile of **Sacré-Coeur** (Sacred Heart) from all over Paris. Its dome is the second highest point in Paris after the Eiffel Tower, and the mosaic of Christ above the main altar is stunning. The dome is vast and, from inside the church, recedes away into darkness. Spectacular views abound from the church's position high on the Montmartre hills—once you get up there. The fit can climb the streets (mostly steps, since many of these streets are too steep for cars), and those who are harboring their energy for other adventures can take the Funiculaire, a sort of vertical railway. There are telescopes on the plaza in front of Sacré-Coeur, but I'd save my 10F for other things: The view is too spectacular to need help. *[35 Rue de Chevalier, 18ᵗʰ; Metro 12: Abbesses. Church free, admission charge for Dome and Crypt.]*

Near the botanical gardens in the Latin Quarter is the hub of Paris's Islamic community, the **Mosquée de Paris** *[Place du Puits de l'Ermite, 5ᵗʰ; Metro 7: Place Monge. Closed Friday and Muslim* *holy days.]* is part of a religious and educational complex with lavishly-decorated domes and mosaics and a slender minaret that towers above the red-tiled roofs of the mosque.

It's a bit out of the way, just beyond the Périphérique, the ring road surrounding Paris, but the history buffs in your family will enjoy a trip to the splendid **Basilique Saint-Denis** *[Rue de la Légion d'Honneur, 93200; Metro 13: Basilique de Saint-Denis. Carte Musées. Under 12 free].* Most of the kings of France were buried here, from Dagobert (d. 639) to Louis XVIII (d. 1824). Not even London's Westminster Abbey has had a longer history of sheltering royal remains. During the revolution, however, the tombs were opened and the remains thrown into unmarked graves. The tombs themselves were restored to the church in the nineteenth century. This is at least the fourth church on this site. The first was built because the early Christian bishop Denis, who was beheaded by the Romans, reputedly picked up his head and walked here, where, apparently, he finally became resigned

St-Germain-l'Auxerrois, an old church near the Louvre

to his fate and allowed himself to be buried. The present church, begun in the twelfth century, is almost as large as Notre Dame.

Two central Paris churches have grim histories, and now possess such quiet beauty that they're worth stopping in if you're nearby. **St-Germain-des-Pres** [*3 Place Saint-Germain-des-Pres, 5*th*; Metro 4: St-Germain-des-Pres Free.*] is the oldest parish in Paris, dating from the year 542. In 1792 more than 300 people were hacked to death near here by the mob. Even worse was the massacre at **St-Germain l'Auxerrois** [*2 Place du Louvre, 1*st*; Metro 1: Louvre, 7 Pont Neuf. Free*]. Thousands of Protestant Huguenots were slaughtered here on August 24, 1572, in the St. Bartholomew's Day Massacre planned by King Charles IX and others. This quiet interior seems such an unlikely place for such horrors.

One more stop. If you are shopping at Les Halles, you must stop at **St-Eustache** [*Place du Jour, 1*st*; Metro 4: Les Halles. Free*]. It's an especially lovely church with a very old feel to it. The main reason, though, is to take a picture of the kids standing in the middle of the gigantic sculpture of a hand and head, looking like they're about to get gobbled up. It's a funny spot, an odd juxtaposition with the sixteenth-century church behind it.

Recommendations

✔ Someone (maybe tired parents, maybe not...) should climb Notre Dame's towers for photos of the distant view and the nearby gargoyles.

✔ Stop occasionally in neighborhood churches you pass. They'll provide quiet moments away from the noise of the street—and chairs or pews to rest your feet.

✔ Pay attention not just to the spectacular church buildings themselves, but to the art and the memorials they contain.

Chapter 13 Highlights

13. The Art of Paris

S aying that Paris is a good place to see art is a lot like saying that Mozart could carry a tune, that Shakespeare could turn a phrase, that Bill Gates has a few dollars. When you talk about ultimates, anything you say sounds like a ridiculous understatement.

Where you go and how much you see of Parisian art museums depends on your family. If kids are too young, or know too little about what they're seeing, their boredom threshold in the average art museum runs about eleven minutes. But if a child is captured by art—the colors, the shapes, the textures—you might be in for a long stay. At least, though, most kids are happy to do a bit of superficial grazing through an art museum to see in person some of the things they've seen in books and on television all their lives.

There are about as many art museums in Paris as there are McDonald's restaurants in New York, but in this chapter we'll poke our heads into the seven that might do the best job of creating some excitement and some memories.

The Big Three

We'll begin with the three most-visited museums in Paris. Each attracts enough visitors every single day to populate a fair-sized city, and each has a collection that's so large that you could spend your whole vacation there and still have a sense of not really having seen it in much depth. Each contains countless works of art that even the youngest member of your family will recognize, and they'll love going back to school and talking about it with worldly sophistication when the teacher mentions it. Let's start with what is probably the most famous museum on Planet Earth.

The Louvre

The Louvre is much more than an art museum. It's a museum of civilization, tracing the symbols of humanity back to their prehistoric beginnings. To think of the Louvre as merely (if you can say "merely" about its thousands of wondrous works) galleries of paintings, you're missing most of its collection! Besides painting, there are six other important collections housed here, including sculpture, Egyptian antiquities, Greek and Roman artifacts, Oriental and Islamic art, and more.

Tip: Getting in is the biggest problem. Lines at the pyramid entrance in the summer can be more than an hour long just to buy a ticket. Holders of the Carte Musées and other advance tickets can go to a special entrance in Passage Richelieu under the arch of the building just north of the pyramid. Lines are much shorter. If you don't have the Carte Musées, there's also an entrance beneath the triumphal arch at the end of the plaza west of the pyramid, and another on the street that runs north of the Louvre, at 99 Rue de Rivoli where lines are shorter.

When you enter the museum, you're actually one floor underground, on a level with shopping and restaurants. Beneath the great glass pyramid are escalators that will carry you to the exhibition areas on the

The Louvre, center of the world of art

ground, first, and second floors of the three wings of the museum.

Pick up a map as you enter, available in seven languages, and if you plan to see the museum thoroughly, you can get an audioguide in six languages. Most travel guides recommend at least three to four hours for a cursory trip through the Louvre. Do that if you want, but only if everyone agrees. That's an awfully long time in a museum, even as spectacular a museum as the Louvre. You can't possibly see it all, even in four hours, so there's no point in half the people in your group being miserable. If some want to see more and some are ready to move on, it might be a good time to split up and meet later near the ice cream vendor just past the arch in the Jardin de Tuileries.

What do you want to see here? Probably everyone will want to see the most famous painting of all, the *Mona Lisa*. It's in Gallery 6 on the 1st floor of the Denon wing of the museum. There are signs with Mona's picture on them pointing the way, but here's the quickest way to get there: Enter through the

Denon access and walk straight to the elevators next to Gallery 1. (If you get to the Roman gallery with windows overlooking the courtyard, you've passed them.) Take one of the elevators to the 1st floor. (Americans, remember that's one above the ground floor.) When you get out, you're right outside Gallery 6.

Probably the next most famous artwork at the Louvre is the famous armless lady, the *Venus de Milo*. If that's your next stop, go

> ***Tip:*** *The Louvre is much less crowded at night. Parts of the museum are open on Mondays until 9:45 pm and the entire museum is open Wednesdays until the same time. Admission is free for students under 18 but reduced-price tickets are available after 3 pm and on Sundays. The Louvre is free for everyone on the first Sunday of each month.*

out the same doorway you went in to Gallery 6, near the elevators. Turn right, going through Gallery 75 (large French paintings) and go down the stairs straight ahead. (You'll see the famous headless statue *Winged Victory* as you do.) When you reach the next level, the ground floor, enter the Sully wing of the Louvre. You'll pass through Galleries 4, 5, and 6; keep going straight to 8. When you reach Gallery 12, there's Venus, waiting for you with open ar—... no, perhaps, not. There's also a nice exhibition there about what the complete statue *might* have looked like.

Every visitor wants to see the Mona Lisa

Straight on from Venus is the spectacular Egyptian collection, and going down one more flight of stairs from there will take you underground again to the fortified walls of the medieval fortress of the original Louvre.

There's too much to choose from. We'll leave you here. The free map is excellent and will get you to the sort of art or famous masterpieces that most interest you. *[The Louvre has (and needs) no street address, 1ˢᵗ; Metro 1: Louvre Rivoli, 7: Musée du Louvre. Closed Tuesday. Carte Musées. Under 18 free.]*

Musée d'Orsay

You know, of course, of the French Revolution of 1789, in which the king, the queen, and several thousand of their closest friends lost their heads. Little more than a half century later, there was *another* revolution in France that changed the artistic landscape forever—Impressionism. The Orsay, a fabulous museum in a converted railway station, is the national museum of Impressionist and Post-Impressionist art. If your taste runs toward that artistic genre, entering here is like entering the Holy Land must be for the devout.

You enter into a vast sunlit sculpture court under the great glass roof of the old station, lined by galleries of painting and decorative arts. The middle level has more sculpture, including the Rodin Court at the rear, with important works by that master.

The great body of the painting collection is on the upper level, with breathtaking rooms full of the works of Monet, Renoir, Degas, Cézanne, and others. You'll recognize many of the works from books and reproductions—but these are the genuine articles.

Near the café or near Gallery 28, the kids will enjoy looking through the back of one of the gigantic station clocks, and adjacent to the café is a pleasant outdoor terrace with a spectacular view of the Seine and the Louvre beyond. Maps and guidebooks are available in many languages. *[62 Rue de Lille, 7ᵗʰ;*

Metro 12: Solférino; RER C: Musée d'Orsay. Closed Monday. Carte Musées. Under 18 free.]

Musée National d'Art Moderne

Remember the Pompidou Center, the building with its guts hanging out? It's home to the Museum of Modern Art, now entirely reopened after a lengthy refurbishment. Kids will often like this museum better than more traditional galleries like the Louvre or the Orsay because the art is much more varied and unconventional—cubist, expressionistic, abstractionist, minimalist, pop, op, and every other twentieth-century approach is represented here. *[Place Georges-Pompidou, 4ᵗʰ; Metro 11: Rambuteau. Closed Tuesday. Carte Musées. Under 16 free]*

Modern and Surreal

If the kids have a penchant for unusual art, there's a place in Montmartre, one of the most charming sections of Paris, that will make them go wild, **Espace Montmartre Salvador Dali**. Here is a museum devoted entirely to the great Spanish surrealist. *[11 Rue Poulbot, 18ᵗʰ; Metro 12: Abbesses.]* If you're visiting the basilica of Sacré-Coeur, leave the plaza by the west, pass the old church of St. Pierre de Montmartre, and follow the street that runs along the north side of the picturesque Place du

Tertre, which will be crowded with artists. Follow the street as it curves down and to the left, and you'll reach the museum near the end of the street.

Upstairs is a bookstore and gift shop with an

Find some time for the Dali Museum assortment of strange items,

including a book about Dali's famous moustache. Downstairs the real fun begins, with hundreds of weird and wonderful Dali artworks in every imaginable medium. My own favorite is the artist's personal interpretation of classical sculpture, *Venus à la Girafe*. In the background, music plays, along with the sound of Dali's own voice. The museum will give everyone a new way of looking at familiar things and is a sure-fire discussion starter about the nature of art.

For something more conventionally unconventional, visit the **Musée Picasso**. *[Hôtel Salé, 5 Rue de Thirigny, 4th; Metro 1: St-Paul Closed Tuesday. Carte Musées. Under 18 free]*. The museum is housed in an exceptional building in its own right, a splendid seventeenth-century mansion. Note the reliefs above its grand main staircase and the iron chandelier above. The museum houses Picasso's own collection of his work, with pieces covering his career from 1905 to 1973, both painting and sculpture. There are works here by contemporaries of Picasso, as well. Kids might enjoy the oddity of the approaches for a while. Almost everything is in French, but that's the beauty of art—language doesn't matter. Enter the gate and turn right for tickets; the entrance is in center of the courtyard.

Two More Favorites

If your group would like to sample Impressionism without the large scale of the Orsay, there's a wonderful small museum that's often overlooked by visitors in a rush to get to the more famous ones. This is the **Musée l'Orangerie des Tuileries** *[Jardin des Tuileries, 1st; Metro 7, 14: Concorde. Closed Tuesday. Carte Musées. Under 18 free]*. This was the most important museum of Impressionism until the Orsay opened in 1986. It's much smaller and much more manageable. It's even possible to go at a leisurely pace, see the entire collection, and be finished in well under the Lain two-hour museum limit. All the great

Impressionists are represented here, but Renoir and Monet are given the most space. The pride of the museum is in the lower level—eight enormous water lily murals by Monet. The museum is at the Concorde end of the gardens, along the Seine.

Last stop on our artistic tour is one that will fascinate almost everybody. Sculpture is a very approachable art form, and no modern sculptor (some would say no sculptor ever) has been able to reach his audience the way Auguste Rodin has. Many of his most famous works are in a beautiful eighteenth-century

The Rodin Museum is home to the sculptor's greatest works

mansion in Invalides in the **Musée Rodin** [*77 Rue de Varenne, 7ᵗʰ; Metro 13: Varenne. Closed Monday. Carte Musées. Under 18 free.*] You can see well-known pieces like *The Thinker, The Kiss,* and *Eve* in the mansion itself, and the garden adjacent to the house, so loved by the sculptor, is filled with bronzes of his work.
The museum also contains paintings by luminaries like Van Gogh, Monet, and Renoir.

Oh, there's more, much more art in Paris. We've barely started, and we're already at the end of the chapter. But there's one more stop you might make.

Since Paris is the city of art, a fabulous memento of your trip might be some original art to take home. You can find artists and art students at work throughout Paris. You'll find them at the Place du Tertre near the Dali Museum, and they fill the plaza and streets near Notre Dame. None of these artists is likely to end up with work hanging in the Louvre, but you might find an original scene of a favorite Paris site that will bring back memories for years to come—and for very little money. For just a bit more, you'll have no trouble finding one of the artists to do a charcoal or pastel drawing of your family. What a special souvenir of such a special trip!

Recommendations

✔ Paris is the world's foremost city of art. You ought to visit at least one art museum. Let the kids decide which one.

✔ Before your trip, get an art book from your local library and find some of the famous paintings from Paris museums, then seek out the originals when you get there. Or find artists' views of Paris you especially like, then try to locate the places where the artists stood to make the paintings. Activities like these make art come alive for children—*and* adults.

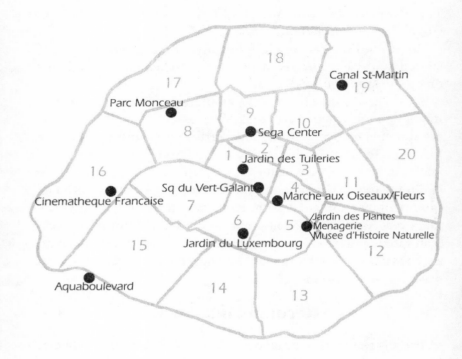

Chapter 14 Highlights

14. Parks and Diversions

Paris is a city of beauty, but it's a beauty we usually associate with graceful buildings and monumental architecture. Ah, *mon cheri*, there is *natural* beauty in profusion as well, lush green spaces pretty as postcards. There are flowers, animals and waterways to admire. And when you want something a bit different, well, Paris has that, too.

In the Jardin des Plantes

The Jardin des Plantes (botanical gardens) and the Musée National d'Histoire Naturelle (natural history museum) hold a treasure house of attractions that are seldom on the must-see lists of tourists. There are few places in the world, however, that can rival this 28-hectare (69-acre) complex for its variety of views into the natural world, and it's an easy place to spend an entire day. The only drawback is that each attraction has a separate admission charge of about 30F. Even with reduced rates for students, it can be an expensive day if everyone goes to every attraction. Fortunately, there are so many things to do here that it's a perfect place for your group to split up so each person can spend more time with the things he or she would like. Most of the attractions make little provision for visitors who don't read French, but most displays are clear and just a bit of time and an inexpensive dictionary will be all the help you need. *[57 Rue Cuvier, 5th; Metro 10: Jessieu; RER C: Gare d'Austerlitz. Garden and Zoo open daily, most museums closed Tuesday. Garden free but separate admission charges for most attractions].*

The Park and Gardens

One of the most pleasant places Paris offers on a sunny day is the esplanade through the Jardin des Plantes. This half-kilometer-long promenade near the east (Austerlitz) entrance is a comfortable place to stroll and play and to forget the traffic just beyond the trees. On one side of the walks are the buildings of the natural history museum; on the other side are the botanic gardens and zoo.

If you come in the west (Jessieu) entrance, you'll find things

The Ménagerie is popular with Parisians and visitors alike

more wooded, but with a tall hill sticking up in the center. Before you wander over to the esplanade, head toward the hill and try your luck in the labyrinth. If you find your way through, you'll be rewarded with a great view of the park from the gazebo at the top of the hill. The maze is both fun—and free.

Greenhouses display plant life from every corner of the Earth. Kids inevitably gasp at their first glimpse of the tropical house and the enormous fronds looking like they want to escape or like something out of *Little Shop of Horrors*; it's fun to stand there and watch people's reaction for a few minutes. There's a small charge, about 15F, to enter the greenhouse, but just wandering about, looking at the variety of plants and trees is fun. The garden was originally set up in the 1620s to raise medicinal plants for the king, but it's been open to Parisians for more than 350 years. The oldest tree in Paris is here, as well as exotic trees from around the world.

The Ménagerie

The zoo at Vincennes is larger and more modern, but this, the oldest zoo in France, is my favorite Paris zoo. You can see it in an hour or so, and can get

> ***Tip:*** *If anyone in your group likes chocolate ice cream, stop at the snack bar near the zoo entrance. The richness and smoothness of the chocolat nuit defies description.*

closer to the animals than is possible in more modern zoos— just a couple of arm-lengths from some very genuine lions, for example. The layout is a bit old-fashioned, and the little effort to display animals in their natural habitats is in the vivarium, where the displays change periodically.

Musée National d'Histoire Naturelle

This nice complex of five museums has something for everyone in settings from the modern to the old-fashioned. The show-

Protected Species

The *Ménagerie* has a particular specialty in reptiles, insects, and microscopic life. Microscopes are provided in the rotunda in the center of the zoo to display the sorts of creatures we never see with our naked eyes.

Maybe this special interest in such unusual creatures is just a way for the zoo to protect its exhibits. When Paris was besieged by the Prussian army in 1871, food supplies in Paris ran out. Thousands of people starved to death during the siege and the situation was desperate. Hungry Parisians ended up at the zoo and most of the animals in the zoo ended up on Parisian dinner tables.

Perhaps the curators decided that such a raid was less likely to happen if they became known not only for their lions and monkeys, but also for their iguanas, caterpillars, and microbes.

piece is the **Grande Galerie de l'Évolution.** Although the museum dates back to 1889, it was closed for nearly thirty years beginning in 1965, and its approach was completely re-thought. The new museum is one of the most modern and comprehensive natural history museums in the world. Exhibitions cover all types of living beings from all climates, with special emphasis on change, development, and adaptation. The exhibits are exciting but the most fascinating part is the *Galerie des Espèces Disparues*—the Gallery of Extinct Species. This may be the only chance you ever have to lay eyes on animals that have died out completely, like the Tasmanian Devil. Many of these preserved specimens are the last ones remaining on Earth.

The museum complex also contains the **Galerie de Minéralogie**, with an outstanding collection of minerals, crystals, and meteorites, and careful attention to radioactive elements. The **Galerie Paléontologique** has a vast collection of fossils of all types. What that museum does for animal life, the **Galerie de Paléobotanique** does for plants, with extensive exhibits on the development of plant life on Earth. The **Galerie Entomologique** focuses on insects, both contemporary and fossilized.

Paris is filled with natural wonders. For a more informal look at animals and plants than you get in settings like this, it's fun to browse through the pet shops along the **Quai de la Mégisserie** across from the Conciergerie. There's an irony in that, since before the Revolution, this was where the slaughterhouses were located. Now the animals here, both domestic and exotic, are intended for companionship rather than supper.

Walk past the pet shops on the Quai de la Mégisserie

For flowers intended for a glass vase, instead of a glass case (as in a few of the places above) you can't do better than to visit the **Marché aux Fleurs** (flower market) on the Ile de la Cité at the end of the Pont Notre-Dame. There's a beautiful variety of flowers there six days a week. More fun for the kids, though, is the *seventh* day. Every Sunday the flower market becomes the **Marché aux Oiseaux**—the bird market. It's just as colorful and a lot noisier than the flower market, and worth some time if you're visiting any of the Ile de la Cité attractions on a Sunday.

Other Parks and Gardens

The large central parks of Paris seem almost to exist for the view more than for active recreation. The views *are* extraordinary and, don't worry—there's plenty to keep you occupied in the parks.

The most impressive straight line on the planet might be the one that begins at the great glass pyramid that serves as the entrance to the Louvre. Go northwest from there and you will travel beneath Napoleon's Arc de Triomphe du Carrousel, through the center of the Jardin des Tuileries, across Place de la Concorde and the Obelisk, up the Avenue Champs Élysées to the great Arc de Triomphe and straight to the mammoth la Grande Arche at La Defense. Wow!

The Arc de Triomphe du Carrousel stands between the Louvre and the Tuileries

If they are going to be part of an array like this, the **Jardin des Tuileries** [*Metro 1: Tuileries; 1, 8, 12: Concorde*] had better be something special. They are a delight. These formal gardens are the site of a formal royal palace built in the mid-1500s. It was destroyed in the riots of 1871. The small (at least when compared with the more famous one up the street) triumphal arch was built in 1805 to commemorate the conquests of the Emperor Napoleon. The gardens have broad parkways for running and shady walks for strolling. The biggest drawback is that you have to stay off the grass.

Fortunately there's a lot to do off the grass.

During the summer there's usually a Fun Fair with a Ferris wheel and other assorted rides and games along the north edge of the park. At all times of the year you can find a carousel, pony and donkey rides, a children's playground, trampolines, and plenty of things to eat that have absolutely no nutritional value. Probably the most popular spot is near the central fountain. For about 10F for a half-hour, generations of children have rented small boats to sail in the fountain. It's as popular today as it was in their great-grandparents' day.

The gardens have concession stands offering a variety of snacks and meals, and there are public toilets at the end of the park near the Place de la Concorde.

Many people consider the most beautiful gardens in Paris to be the **Jardin du Luxembourg** *[RER B: Luxembourg]*. I wouldn't argue the proposition. The view here stretches from the Palais du Luxembourg on the north—the home of the French Senate—to the Observatoire de Paris, the observatory where the size of the solar system was first calculated and where the planet Neptune was discovered. Here, too, you can find children boating on the central lake, and there are puppet shows on weekend afternoons. The orchard contains more than 200 types of apple and pear trees. There's a wonderful playground here if you have small children. It costs a few francs, but it's worth it.

The Ile de la Cité has two small parks that are worth checking out, not because there's anything to do there, but because they are postcard pretty. The **Square du Vert-Galant** is at the westernmost tip of the island and has one of the most gorgeous

Kids have been sailing boats in the Tuileries fountains for decades

views in all Paris, straight down the Seine with landmarks galore in your field of vision. Cross the road above the square (the Pont Neuf) and walk between the buildings on Rue Henri Robert and you'll find yourself in **Place Dauphine**. Trees line the triangular plaza and you'll feel like you've stepped into an Impressionist painting. It's one place in Paris that is probably even prettier in winter than in summer. *[Metro 7: Pont Neuf]*

For an afternoon picnic of bread and cheese in central Paris, the place of choice might be **Parc Monceau** *[Boulevard de Courcelles, 17th; Metro 2: Monceau]*. This looks like a park that's slipped out of some landscaper's fairy tale, filled with monuments and architectural oddities that don't have any relation to each other but, strangely, seem to fit together. Here is a colonnade, there a waterfall, nearby a pyramid, an obelisk, a pagoda. The park is a favorite of Parisians but tourists seldom visit here. There's no place more congenial for resting travel-weary feet, however.

Place Dauphine looks like an Impressionist painting

Afloat

Sooner or later you'll be tired of walking, but not of sightseeing. The solution is simple: Do your sightseeing sitting down. The best way is by boat. The River Seine, as it passes through central Paris, offers some of the richest eye candy on Earth—it can't be overstated. You have several choices for your river trip. Here are a few. **Bateaux-mouches** *[departs from the Pont de l'Alma on the Right Bank; Metro 9: Alma-Marceau]* and **Bateaux Parisiens Tour Eiffel** *[departs from the Pont d'Léna on the Left Bank; Metro 6, 9: Trocadéro; RER C: Champ de Mars-Tour Eiffel]* ply their way up and down the river all year long. From April to September, **Batobus** stops at several places

> ***Tip:*** *For the most spectacular view of this spectacular city, take the tour at night, when the buildings are brightly lit. Tour boats carry their own floodlights, too, and illuminate the buildings in brilliant fashion as they pass by.*

between the Eiffel Tower and Notre Dame Cathedral. Passengers buy a ticket that is good for the whole day and can get on and off

You can float boats—only boats—in several parks

at will. A one-day ticket is 60F, and a 2-day ticket is 90F. Children under 12 are half-price. **Bateaux Parisiens** also runs summertime tours from the Quai de Montebello facing Notre Dame. Tours are in glass-roofed boats with commentary in several languages.

For a more serene trip, try the canal. From the Parc de la Villette (Chapter 17) you can take a boat to the Bassin de la Villette marina *[Metro 2, 5, 7: Jaurés]*, where several companies run a 2- to 3-hour trip to the Porte de l'Arsenal near the Bastille *[Metro 1, 5, 8: Bastille]*.

A Few Diversions

While it doesn't seem at first to make much sense to travel to Paris to do something you can do at home, long-stay visitors faced with a rainy day might take in a movie at the **Cinémathèque Française** *[Palais de Chaillot, 16*th*; Metro 6, 9: Trocadéro]*. This is the place to see classic films in their original language. The program changes daily.

Video gamers can get their fill at the **Micromania Sega Center** *[3 Boulevard des Italiens 2*nd*; Metro 3, 8: Richelieu-Drouot. Closed Monday. Open until 12:30 AM Sunday-Thursday, 2 AM Friday and Saturday]*. Every imaginable Sega game is here from video to virtual reality. To make the experience complete, there's even a McDonald's inside. Might be a good place for the kids if Mom and Dad want to shop in the Passages and department stores nearby (or for Dad, too, while Mom shops....)

A fun summertime afternoon might involve a visit to **Aquaboulevard** *[4 Rue Louis Armand, 15*th*; Metro 8: Balard]*. This large waterpark has pools, water slides, wave pools, artificial beaches, and indoor games and recreation. It's open until 11 PM; parents and one child cost about 100F, with a charge of about 35F for each additional child.

Recommendations

✔ A half day or more visiting the attractions in the Jardin des Plantes provides something for everyone.

✔ Don't shy away from some attractions just because you don't speak or read French. Exhibits are usually clear and looking up a few key words in a simple dictionary normally provides all the direction you need.

✔ Take a boat trip, the best way to let everyone rest and sightsee at the same time.

✔ Plan a picnic in a park some afternoon or evening. You can't be on the go all the time, and a chance for your family to relax together under a cool tree and talk about the trip is something that's hard to beat.

For the latest updates to *Paris for Families*, check our page on the Web at:

www.interlinkbooks.com/parisforfamilies.html

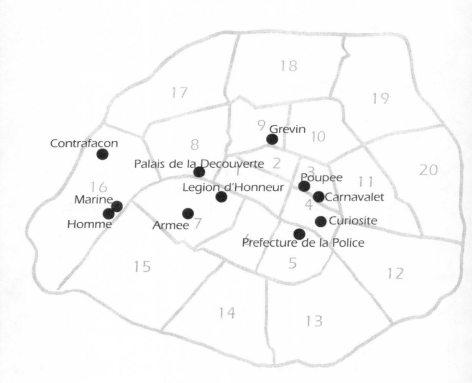

Chapter 15 Highlights

15. Museum Potpourri

A really compulsive visitor could probably go to all the museums in Paris, but it would take determination, endurance, and the complete lack of a life for months—perhaps years. By Chapter 15 in the book you ought to have a few other ideas for your trip besides spending every waking moment in front of a glass case or a picture frame.

Still, everybody has a special interest, and there's a pretty good chance that Paris has an exhibition devoted to it somewhere. Chapter 15 will profile twelve specialized museums that might just strike a chord with a member of your family. Here are a dozen fascinating somethings to consider.

It's appropriate that we start with the museum of the city of Paris, the **Musée Carnavalet** [*23 Rue de Sévigné, 3ʳᵈ; Metro 1: Saint-Paul. Closed Monday. Carte Musées. Under 18 free.*] Perhaps not surprisingly, there's not a lot of help here for non-speakers of French, but it doesn't matter a whit. This luxurious mansion is packed full of artifacts that are self-explanatory, or accompanied by signs that are easy to decipher with a simple dictionary. One of the neatest exhibits is of scale models of Paris, mostly the Ile de la Cité, at various times in history. There's also a dazzling goldsmith's shop from the Rue Royal on the first floor. (Reminder for Americans: That's one flight up from street level.)

One of the most charming museums in Paris is the doll museum, the **Musée de la Poupée** *[Impasse Berthaud, 3rd; Metro 11: Rambuteau. Closed Monday]*. It's not easy to find. You have to walk down an unlikely-looking cul-de-sac on the east side of Rue Beaubourg, just north of Rue Rambuteau. When this improbable alleyway turns suddenly to the left, you see the museum at the end of the street, cute as a button. Or you can just follow the almost constant procession of little girls and their mothers or grandmothers—or often all three generations together. Fathers are scarce here. (When I've visited here alone, I've gotten some odd looks—but that happens to me a lot anyway.) French is the only language used here, but nowhere in Paris does language matter less.

The museum couldn't be more perfect. It's snug and warm, and scaled to a size that isn't intimidating to small folks. You can't count on this all the time, perhaps, but sometimes the very first thing you see as you open the door is a basket of kittens, wriggling into the best position under their mother for an afternoon snack; every little girl who comes through the door squeals with delight. The museum is a wonderland of dolls by the hundred—china dolls, wooden dolls, fabric dolls. Many of the antique dolls date back to the mid-nineteenth century, and the sumptuous doll clothes attract as much attention as the dolls themselves. If there's a little girl who loves dolls in your group, she'll remember this place more than the Eiffel Tower.

A few blocks away is a museum that's mostly fathers and sons, although the other gender is, at least, more than nominally represented. This is the museum of magic, the **Musée de la Curiosité** *[11 Rue St-Paul, 4th; Metro 1: St-Paul or 7: Sully Morland. Open only on Wednesday, Saturday, and Sunday afternoons]*. This museum is another one that's easy to miss because it's down a flight of stairs in a cavernous basement. Look on the west side of the street. Although this little museum shows you how magic tricks work, it doesn't demystify the art at all. Even after you see how tricks work with mirrors, springs, and hidden drawers, you're just as amazed as ever when you see them performed. A half-hour magic show is presented regularly on the museum's small stage, and the man in the gift shop usually gives an impromptu magic show as he demonstrates the shop's many props and tricks. This is another place where it doesn't matter whether you speak French. You'll be amazed in any language. Notwithstanding the museum's posted opening hours, if you're in the area on other days, you might be lucky and find it open, as I have once or twice.

Since it's in a major police station on the Left Bank, you might expect security to be tight at the police museum, the **Musée de la Préfecture de la Police** *[4 Rue de la Mountain, 5ʰ; Metro 10: Maubert-Mutualité. Closed Sunday. Free].* Rather surprisingly, though, nobody seems to mind having you wander around in police headquarters. Ask at the information desk for the

It's actually quite easy to visit the Police Museum

museum and you'll be directed to an elevator for the second floor, and no one checks to make sure that's where you go (not that you'd want to go anywhere else—there are just generic offices in all directions).

The museum is an interesting collection of weapons, restraint devices, uniforms, and memorabilia from the Paris police, and a history of the most notorious underworld characters in Paris. The ability to read a little French would be an asset here to get the meaning and extent of the exhibits and documents, but most of the collection is accessible even with just a bit of facility with that well-thumbed dictionary. The street is hard to find on most maps. It's off Rue St-Geneviève, which runs between Rue des Écoles and Boulevard St-Germain. The building is the ugly modern one on the west side of the street.

Do you have a coin collector in your group? Consider a visit to the **Musée de la Monnaie** *[11 Quai de Conti, 6ᵗʰ; Metro 1 ,7: Pont Neuf (across the river) or 4, 10: Odéon. Closed Monday. Carte Musées. Under 16 free].* In what was once the chief mint in France, visitors can see coins and medals from ancient times to the present. There's a good display showing how coins are made and rare pieces that really illustrate the history of France in miniature. Sorry: No free samples.

Tip: *If you have a stamp collector in your midst, rather than a coin collector, the best place to go is the Avenue de Marigny (between the Champs Élysées and the Palais de l'Élysées) on Sunday. A large stamp and postcard market sets up shop there every week with a huge variety of stamps, envelopes, and other people's mail from around the world.*

When you go to see the Tomb of Napoléon, you might spend an interesting hour or two in the **Musée de l'Armée** *[Hôtel National des Invalides, 129 Rue de Grenelle, 7ᵗʰ; Metro 8, 13; RER C: Invalides. Carte Musées. Under 12 free].* Walk across the cobbled courtyard beneath the battle flags and inspect the cannons, and you almost expect to hear the clatter of hoofs as the king's musketeers ride in through the gate. This place looks exactly the way you think a seventeenth-century military garrison ought to. The galleries that surround the courtyard are like a Hollywood prop room. There are countless colorful uniforms, banners, drums, muskets and all the wherewithal of Napoléonic warfare. In fact, much of the collection is devoted to Napoléon, including his uniforms, sword, and famous "sideways" hat.

The Army Museum surrounds a cobbled parade ground

The museum is not just limited to that, however. You can find weapons and armor from prehistoric times through World War II, including a remarkable collection of helmets and suits of armor from the Middle Ages.

More reflections of military glory can be found at the **Musée de la Legion d'Honneur** *[2 Rue de Bellechasse, 7th; Metro 12: Solférino; RER C: Musée d'Orsay. Closed Monday. Carte Musées. Under 16 free].* This museum, which is straight across from the entrance to the Musée d'Orsay, commemorates winners of the

Legion of Honor, France's highest military decoration, and has displays covering more than 900 years of medals and the trappings of orders of chivalry. Another of Napoléon's swords is here as well.

A great excuse to visit the Grand Palais is a stop in the west wing of the building, the **Palais de la Découverte** *[Avenue Franklin D. Roosevelt, 8ᵗʰ; Metro 1,9: Franklin D. Roosevelt. Closed Monday]*. The exhibition was originally built for the 1937 World's Fair to demonstrate the principles of science, and it's still serving that function in the twenty-first century. The material is more explanatory than experiential like the many hands-on displays at the Cité des Science (Chapter 17) but there are good displays of the foundations of physics, mathematics, computer science, and so on. The exhibition also includes a fine planetarium (extra charge).

People either love wax museums or they hate them. If someone from your family insists on a wax museum, you're in luck with the **Musée Grévin** *[16 Boulevard Montmartre, 9ᵗʰ; Metro 8, 9: Grands Boulevards]*. The usual suspects all are here—the president of France, the president of the United States, the Pope, British prime minister, German chancellor, and assorted European royalty past and present. The history of France is, as you'd naturally assume, well represented with tableaux of Napoléon, Louis XVI and Marie-Antoinette, Voltaire, Joan of Arc, Victor Hugo, and all manner of other kings and historical figures. But although the pop culture figures on display depend a lot on who's hot at the moment, you might look for Madonna, Michael Jackson, Laurel and Hardy, Charlie Chaplin, Gina Lollobrigida, Charlton Heston, Elizabeth Taylor, Clark Gable, Marilyn Monroe, and countless others. Some of the figures look very lifelike and others are less successful, but if you're into this sort of thing, it can be a fun stop, and lines are not as long or prices quite as high as Madam Tussaud's in London. It does seem to be successful: The museum has been here since 1885 and claims to have had 50 million visitors.

Paris has a museum devoted to counterfeiting, the **Musée de la Contrefaçon** [*16 Rue de la Faisanderie, 16th; Metro 2: Port Dauphine; RER C: Avenue Foch. Closed Saturday. Open afternoons only, except Friday when it is open only in the morning*]. It has nothing to do with the Musée de la Monnaie, however. This is the sort of counterfeiting Paris takes really seriously: fashion and accessories! Can you tell the *real* Dior gown from the fake? Tell the difference between genuine Chanel perfume and the knockoff? (Hint: If you've bought it from a guy selling perfume in 2-liter bottles from the trunk of his car outside a football stadium, it's probably not the real thing.) *If* you can find this small museum open, it's a brief but interesting stop.

One of the nicest and most accessible anthropological museums you're likely to find is in the **Palais de Chaillot** across from the Eiffel Tower—the **Musée de l'Homme** [*17 Place du*

The Palais de Chaillot across from the Eiffel Tower has several fine museums

Trocadéro, 16th; Metro 6, 9: Trocadéro. Closed Tuesday.] This fine museum tells the story of human development and social customs from around the world, dealing with both ordinary and exotic things like tattooing, piercings (not sure if those are as exotic today as the museum curators thought when they opened the museum), shrunken heads, funerary practices, clothing, and more. There is an excellent selection of crafts and artworks, and a famous collection of musical instruments from throughout the world. Don't go if you're shy of nudity, since the museum tells the story of human development like it really is. There's little help here for the person who doesn't read or speak French, but most of the exhibits are self-explanatory, and it's worth puzzling out the inscriptions on those that aren't.

If yours is a nautical family, there's another museum in the Palais de Chaillot that you shouldn't miss, the **Musée de la Marine** *[17 Place du Trocadéro, 16th; Metro 6, 9: Trocadéro. Closed Tuesday. Carte Musées. Under 8 free].* This is the oldest nautical museum in the world and has wonderful displays devoted to oceanic search and rescue, ancient ships, modern naval warfare, merchant marine, lighthouses, naval battles during the Napoléonic wars and American Revolution—It's an impressive array. Best of all are the boats themselves: replicas and scale models both large and small of historic craft. It's great fun and very well done.

Paris offers museums for every taste and interest, from erotic art (Sorry. Not in this book.) to mineralogy. There are countless more places than this chapter, or this book, can include. Keep your eyes open as you roam the streets of the city because you're apt to stumble across them almost anywhere. Don't be reluctant to turn aside for a look; remember that being surprised is one of the most delightful parts of traveling.

Recommendations

✔ After you visit a specialized museum like the ones in this chapter, talk about what you saw and discovered. Reinforcement is the key to learning.

✔ Look for attractions in the same area so people who really *don't* want to visit a particular attraction have a nearby alternative. (But, look—if you're a 250-pound, 17-year-old shot-putter, maybe the last place you want to be seen is the doll museum. Trust me: you'll enjoy it, at least for a little while, if you let yourself.)

✔ Keep your passport with you. It serves as the perfect proof of age when you seek free or reduced-price admission. Don't forget to take advantage of those freebees.

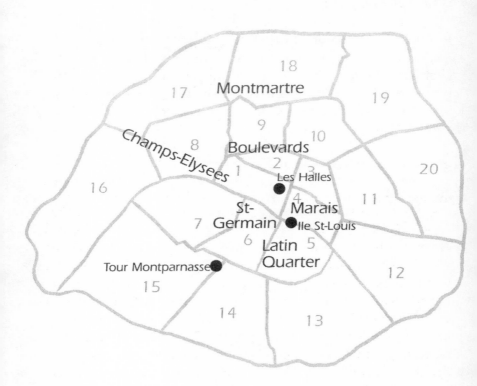

Chapter 16 Highlights

16. Walking and Shopping

W alk. If you really want to get well acquainted with a place, you have to walk as much as you can; that advice has probably come through in almost every chapter. Mostly until now, though, you've been looking for specific attractions. In this chapter, though, the focus will be just to encourage you to explore some particular parts of Paris.

As it happens, all of these places are not only delightful to walk through, but they're very well suited for doing the sort of souvenir shopping—or serious shopping—that some members of your group have been looking forward to ever since you decided to take the trip. Each of these areas has a Parisian "feel" to it that makes you imagine you've slipped into a travelogue, and there are special surprises to be discovered in each.

Le Marais

Centuries ago this area was a swamp, and even a few decades ago, this was not a section of Paris that held any attraction for the visitor. Today, however, the Marais is clean, safe, and very fashionable, without being expensive. If you're looking for unspoiled Paris with old buildings and narrow, winding streets, you can find it in the Marais.

Heart of the district is the **Place des Vosges**, the oldest public square in Paris, completed early in the seventeenth century. *[Metro 1: St-Paul; 5, 8: Bastille]* Colonnaded all around its beautiful 450-year-old buildings, the square itself is a pretty park for picnicking and strolling, much more pleasant family activities than the jousting and dueling that took place here centuries ago. There's a nice children's playground and sandbox, and lovely fountains to sit beside. Under the arches of the buildings are dozens of cafés, restaurants, and boutiques and a couple of luscious chocolatiers. It's also one of the best places to see street entertainers, most of them quite good. The colonnade provides wonderful acoustics! You can visit the house of Victor Hugo, who wrote *Les Misérables* here, at No. 6. (Frankly, the entrance of the house next door at No. 4—not so carefully restored—looks more in keeping with the historic character of the square.)

The Places des Vosges is the oldest and prettiest public square in Paris

Rue de Rosiers in the Jewish Quarter is filled with delicious aromas

A bit west of the Place des Vosges is the heart of the Jewish Quarter, the **Rue des Rosiers** *[Metro 1: St-Paul]*. This might be the best-smelling street in Paris, with bakeries, cafés, delis, kosher markets, and restaurants, and every manner of good food packed one next to the other all the way down the street, sometimes interrupted by clothing, jewelry, and religious shops. There's something for everybody here. Not everything is ethnic: You'll also find Ben and Jerry's and Häagen-Daz ice cream shops directly across the street from each other.

Just south is the **Village St-Paul**, a beautifully restored area of narrow little streets and fine antique shopping *[Metro 1: St-Paul]*. The garish neon sign above the street welcoming you to the area does seem a bit at odds with its quaint character, but your best bet anyway is to get off the main street and duck into the little courtyards behind, where you'll find many small shops and far fewer people, as well as little places to sit and sip hot chocolate and rest your feet. Wander into some of the tiny streets like the Rue Charlemagne (The nearby Lycée is one of the oldest schools in Paris) and the Rue du Prévôt, a street so narrow it's barely wide enough for three people to walk abreast.

In the Marais you're just a short walk from the **Place de la Bastille** *[Metro 1, 5, 8: Bastille]*, one-time site of the notorious prison, destroyed during the French Revolution. The anniversary of the storming of the Bastille, July 14, 1789, is the chief French national holiday. All traces of the prison are gone now and a spectacular new opera house sits in the square.

A fifteen-minute walk north up the busy Boulevard Beaumarchais is the famous **Cirque d'Hiver** *[Metro 8 Filles du Calvaire]*. Parisians love the circus and as you wander the city, especially near the edges, don't be surprised to find the Big Top set up. There may be a half-dozen circuses running in Paris at any given time. You'll find full information about them in *Pariscope*.

The Latin Quarter

Wander among the twisting old streets in the Latin Quarter

We've already visited many of the attractions in this busy and colorful part of Paris, but your family scholars will certainly want to walk past **La Sorbonne**, one of the oldest and most famous schools in the world, established in the early thirteenth century. The area includes numerous university buildings, the **Collége de France**, and the church, **Eglise de la Sorbonne** that holds the tomb of Cardinal Richelieu. Start from the Place de la Sorbonne *[Metro 10: Cluny-La Sorbonne]* and walk through the area to see the buildings. Bookstores abound in this area, not surprisingly.

You'll enjoy wandering the streets between the Boulevard St-Germain and the river, east of St-Michel. *[Metro 4, RER B, C: St-Michel]* The **Rue de la Harpe** is quiet during the day but at night is crowded with people dining in its inexpensive restaurants, and street entertainers are everywhere. A narrow cross street,

Rue de la Huchette, still has a medieval feel to it. An impoverished young Corsican named Napoléon Bonaparte once lived a hand-to-mouth existence at No. 10. He later made something of a name for himself. Place Maubert was once a popular spot for burning heretics and executing Protestants. There's no point in naming all the streets through here. There are many of great age and character, as well as some that are over-touristed and over-priced. You'll have no trouble telling the difference.

The Sorbonne is one of the oldest universities in the world

Another great walking and eating street is **Rue Mouffetard** *[Metro 7: Place Monge]*. Its character has hardly changed from the 1500s, although it's crowded now because of its popular food market (daily except Monday). Most of the buildings that line the street are many centuries old and there's plenty of food to nibble as you stroll. If you'd rather sit down to eat, there is a nice selection of cafés at Place de la Contrescarpe at the north end of the street.

Montmartre

Paris is filled with so many lovely places to walk that it's hard to choose. My personal first choice is along the along the Seine... unless it's in the shadow of the Eiffel Tower... except for the days when I'd rather walk the old streets of the Marais... or my other first choice (That's four so far), climbing the steep cobbled streets of Montmartre.

Here is the part of Paris where you expect to round a corner and find Van Gogh and his easel, painting a windmill. Where you expect to find Gene Kelly and Leslie Caron dancing through the streets. Where you pass a café and expect to notice Maurice Chevalier and Herminone Gingold sipping champagne.

We've already been here to see Sacré-Coeur (Chapter 10) and the Salvador Dali museum (Chapter 13). It's worth just wandering in this area, however, with so

---

Free and Easy

Here's one big department store worth a visit—but not necessarily for the shopping. Try **La Samaritaine** *along the Seine at the Pont Neuf. This is where you'll find the best free view in Paris, and you don't even have to climb your legs off to see it!*

Go into the store and take the elevator to the ninth floor. When you get off, turn right and follow the sign that says Panorama. You'll go up a flight of stairs, then a set of 11 steep, twisting steps to the open roof.

The sign says watch your head—Do it! But once you're on the rooftop you can see all of Paris laid out before you. There's a broad railing all the way around that will help you identify what you're looking at. Because the store is right on the river in the center of town, it might be the very best view in Paris.

---

many spots that look straight out of an Impressionist painting. The best approach is to take the Metro *[line 2: Anvers]* to Boulevard de Rocheghouart, a busy shopping street where merchants line the crowded sidewalks with their wares. Here you're at the foot of the steep climb up to the basilica. Or you can take the funiculaire if you want to save your legs. The prettiest parts of Montmartre

Some pets are well suited for Montmartre

are west of the church. **Place du Tertre** is postcard pretty, filled with artists and ringed by cafés, but admittedly much of that bit of local color is for the benefit of the tourists. Still, it's easy to picture old Paris here; the buildings and streets *are* authentically part of old Paris.

The steep streets are fascinating. The residents of Montmartre must have the strongest legs and lungs in Paris. They get a good workout on this terrain. It's easy here to tell the residents from the tourists. The tourists are the puffing, red-faced people.

I recall one rainy Monday afternoon, carefully inching my way down a wet brick street, slippery as ice, knowing that if I lost my footing I probably wouldn't stop rolling 'til I got to the Seine. Suddenly I was passed like I was standing still (which I very nearly was) by a ancient blind man, wielding his red-and-white cane in front of him like a saber, moving at a speed I thought remarkable for his age and with a sure-footedness I didn't have at nineteen. He had probably been careening down that hill in all weather for eighty years.

You can see all of Paris from the rooftop of La Samaritaine

Beyond the Place du Tertre, follow the second street to the left, **Rue Lepic**, to see the last two remaining windmills of the 25 or 30 that once stood on the hills here, when this was a village and local farmers brought their wheat to be ground and their grapes to be crushed. Wander the streets, some too steep for cars and converted to steps in places. You might come across one of the oldest nightclubs in Paris, **Au Lapin Agile** (The Nimble Rabbit). It's through the Place J.B. Clement at the beginning of Rue Lepic, then a couple of blocks up Rue des Saules.

When you're ready to leave the area, look for the decorative **Abbesses** Metro station, one of the few remaining original station entrances. There's usually a carousel there, one of dozens in Paris. If you venture farther down the hill, to Boulevard Clichy you'll find yourself in something of an adult entertainment district, so it's not recommended for families after dark, although it's not an unsafe area—just one where you might feel uncomfortable passing through with your children.

Avenue des Champs-Élysées

Is it possible to go to Paris and not stroll down the Champs-Élysées? This is one of the most famous streets in the world—and one of the most expensive. If you plan to eat or shop in *this* neighborhood, better check the limit on your credit card before you leave home.

The great triumphal parades of Paris, from the return of Napoléon's body from St. Helena in 1840 to the liberation of the city from the Nazis in 1944 to the World Cup celebration in 1998, have taken place right here. Its shops are *tres tres chic* and startlingly expensive. A cup of coffee at one of its sidewalk cafés can cost more than 30F. But it's great to stroll up the broad avenue, coming ever closer to the huge Arc de Triomphe.

You'll see lots of famous product names on this street, although for more exclusive shopping you might turn left down

Avenue Montaigne at the circular **Rond Point**. But sticking to the main thoroughfare, there's plenty of shopping, window and otherwise, to be done. Look at the sheen on the cars in the showrooms of the Peugeot and Mercèdès-Benz dealerships. You'll walk past the famous cabaret Lido at No 116. There's a Virgin Megastore for music at No. 52. If you're hungry, Planet Hollywood is at No. 74. If you're *really* hungry, at No. 42 is the Hippo Citroën (open until 5 AM) where you can get a "Magic Burger XXL" for 70F. Any teenager can make that one disappear.

If you want to avoid the crowds, walk on the south side of the street. But there's no fun in that. However, the main **tourist information center** is over there at No. 127.

Les Grands Boulevards and Grand Shopping

The broad boulevards near the Opéra have long been popular for strolling and displaying the latest finery, a tradition that has continued into this new century. Some of the best-known fashion houses are located near here, and the expensive shops and department stores here have left many a credit card just a smoldering ruin. Still, there's no harm in looking, is there?

You might start at Metro Havre Caumartin *[Line 3, 9]* on Boulevard Haussmann, named for the man who redesigned much of Paris in the nineteenth century. Dedicated shoppers may wish to go no further. At No. 64 is **Le Printemps** ("Springtime"), a Mecca for shoppers since 1865. Go to the sixth floor for a view of its wonderful art nouveau dome, and continue up to its rooftop café. You can see fashion shows every Tuesday at 10 AM.

Just down the street is another, even larger department store, **Galeries Lafayette** at No. 40, also gloriously domed. Don't miss the enormous food hall! Fashion shows here are Wednesdays at 11 AM. Next door is a branch of the British giant **Marks and Spencer**. Not through shopping? Then look for the *passages* or

The Passages are exclusive shopping arcades almost 200 years old

galeries as you walk. These glass-roofed nineteenth-century shopping arcades are filled with boutiques and little cafés. There are many, but try north from the Metro on Rue de Caumartin, near the Grands Boulevards Metro station across from Musée Grévin (The Hard Rock Café is at No. 14, if anyone wants a shirt), and just north of the gardens of the Palais Royal on Petits Champs. They're quaint, delightful places to browse and watch people go by.

South of Boulevard Haussmann at the end of Rue Tronchet is the church of St. Mary Magdalene (**La Madeleine**), surrounded by a broad plaza that's a lively market during the day. At the northeast corner of the plaza is **Fauchon**, one of the world's great gastronomic temples. In a city known for its cuisine, this is its finest, most extensive, and most *expensive* food store. Just browsing through here is exciting, and the exotic delicacies make you think you're in a food museum rather than a food store. Worth a sidetrip and maybe a splurge on an exotic snack.

Other Excursions

It is easy to get so inundated with historic sights and exciting museums that you reach overload. Sometimes all you want is a quiet evening walk. The **Ile St-Louis** is perfect. While its sister island Cité is crowded with attractions, St-Louis is quiet and residential. If you're staying nearby, or just want to escape from the bustle of the Latin Quarter or the Marais for a little while, this is your place. The houses here are old, mostly 200 years or more, and the streets are quiet. Mom and Dad *will* have fantasies of what it would be like to live here. (Fabulous... and unbelievably expensive!) But even if you're not rich, you can have a beautifully rich snack while you're on the island. Stop at **Maison Berthillon** at 31 Rue St-Louis-en-I'lle—that's the street that runs down the center of the island. There is no dispute at all that here is the best ice cream in Paris, incredibly rich and smooth, creamy beyond belief. Have *two* dips.

You can't get enough ice cream at Maison Berthillon

The closest thing you'll find to a North American style shopping mall is the **Forum des Halles** *[Metro 4; RER A, B, D: Les Halles]*. This is a huge, four-level shopping complex of nearly 200 stores and restaurants, as well as an important transportation hub. You'll find the usual chain stores here as well as some local favorites. The kids will probably enjoy wandering around here for a while, and there's a nice garden outside, with a special playground, the Jardin des Enfants, for little ones. This might be a place to do some shopping on a rainy day at the end of your trip. If nothing else, you might enjoy stopping in just to see the place. It's built on the former site of the principal food markets of the city and in the nineteenth century was called "the belly of Paris." Now it's a futuristic-looking complex with tubelike passages that resembles nothing so much as an enormous hamster run.

If you're in the area of the Louvre or Tuileries some afternoon, you might stop in at **Angélina's**. This pretty tearoom at No. 226 Rue de Rivoli has a reputation for serving the best hot chocolate in Paris. There are countless shops and restaurants, mostly upscale, beneath the colonnaded archways of this street.

For a real mix of cafés and restaurants, and some of the most vibrant life of the city, stroll along the Boulevard St-Germain and nearby streets on the left bank. *[Metro 4: St-Germain-des-Prés]* A favorite café of Ernest Hemingway was **Les Deux Magots** at No. 170. Next door at No. 172 is the famous **Café de Flore**, where philosophers Jean-Paul Sartre and Simone de Beauvoir argued out the principles of existentialism. Further east, near where St-Germain passes the Odéon Metro station, is a street called the Rue de l'Ancienne-Comédie. At No. 13 is **Le Procope**, now a pleasant restaurant, but in the 1680s one of the world's first coffee houses. Our last stop on this Left Bank café society trip will take us straight south, through Luxembourg Gardens, to the Boulevard du Montparnasse. At No. 171, across from the Port Royal RER station, is **La Closerie des Lilas**, one of the most famous of all Paris cafés. Lenin and Trotsky planned the Russian Revolution here. Hemingway and F. Scott Fitzgerald talked of literature and read each other their favorite Bible passages here, and Hemingway sat on the terrace and in six weeks wrote *The Sun Also Rises.*

While you're in Montparnasse, walk to the **Tour Montparnasse**, one of the tallest buildings in Europe. Parisians hate this building and claim that its modern, generic-skyscraper look detracts horribly from their beautiful city. But you get a spectacular view of all of Paris from its top, and although the building is almost 100 meters shorter than the Eiffel Tower, native Parisians claim it has the best view in all of Paris. The reason for that, they contend, is because it's the only place in the city where you can't see the Tour Montparnasse blighting the skyline!

Recommendations

✔ Spend some time walking through the Marais, the Latin Quarter, or Montmartre. These archetypical Parisian enclaves are crowded with tourists in places, but also offer quiet walks and charming streets.

✔ Ice Cream at Berthillon: make a point of it.

✔ Take in the view at La Samaritaine. It's the best free view in the city.

✔ Walk in as many neighborhoods as you can; you'll find your own special places.

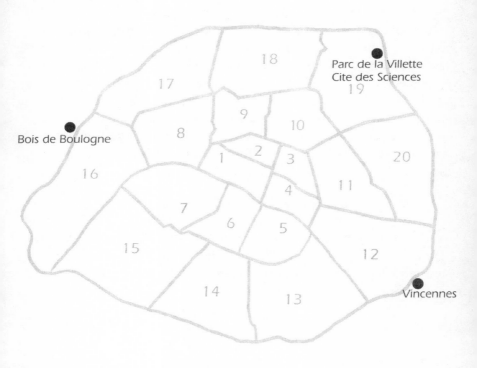

Chapter 17 Highlights

17. Days Out

C entral Paris has so much to see, so much to do—why would you want to get away? Because there's a lot of cool stuff on the outskirts, too.

This chapter will take you to a few places where you can find enough to see and do to keep you busy all day. They make especially ideal outings if you're in Paris for more than a week and want a little variety. As wonderful as central Paris is, it's like eating chocolate—it's delicious and filling, but sometimes you want something else in your diet, too. Well, the places in this chapter are several steps above spinach.

Most are close enough to the city center to make a two- or three-hour excursion perfectly practical if you don't want a full day out; it's just that each has so much to offer that a mere day won't come close to exhausting the possibilities.

Cité des Sciences et de l'Industrie

Don't call this a science museum, because it's not even remotely like any of the things we associate with even the best modern museums.

There are no glass cases, few static displays, no reverential silence. The City of Science and Industry is unique, probably the finest science education facility in the world for children.

The area was once a vast slaughterhouse, supplying meat to all of Paris. Once refrigeration became practical, it was no longer necessary to process meat so close to the consumers it was intended for, and the area languished. But since 1987, the area, now called the Parc de la Villette, has been one of the most amazing cultural centers imaginable. The City of Science is its centerpiece, a science facility that is also a work of art.

Everything in the Cité des Sciences is designed to excite, to educate, to demonstrate. Visitors of all ages can roll up their sleeves and get busy with science, learning for themselves about everything from microbes to galaxies.

Almost everything in the Cité des Sciences is labeled in French, English, German, Spanish, and Italian, and sometimes in Japanese. Interactive computer-based demonstrations are always available in at least French and English and often other languages as well. Headsets with audio guides as well as printed guides to the Cité are available in many languages. Translations are available for most films. The aim is to make things accessible to everybody.

The Cités des Sciences is far more than a museum; it's a great experience

Exhibitions cover both natural and social sciences, with special sections on biology, mathematics, physics, psychology, energy, technology, optics, computer science, geology, health, astronomy, oceanography, ecology—oh, and much more! Each area has demonstrations and displays, and ample opportunity to experiment with the principles presented. Visitors are encouraged to touch and try as much as possible.

There's no way to see the entire building in one trip, because it's hard to go quickly through looking for just highlights. You're sure to get hooked on the section with light games, or finding out about gravitation, or experiencing how mathematical models actually work in real-life applications, and suddenly nearly an hour has somehow slipped away.

This doesn't even begin to cover it!

Outside is the **Géode**, an enormous silver sphere, 36 meters (118 feet) across, the first perfect sphere to be built anywhere in the world. Inside is a huge Imax theater, a 180-degree screen of 1000 square meters (11,000 sq. ft.), where you can see breathtaking films about the climbing of Mount Everest, about the creation of movie special effects like those in *Star Wars*, about space exploration, about roller coasters and other thrill rides. After an experience like this, you'll never be

The Géode is both a movie theater and a work of art

happy with your neighborhood cinema again.

Or you can visit the **Cinaxe**, a movie theater that actually moves on hydraulic jacks, adding a degree of realism that takes the films to the level of virtual reality. The experiences can be intense. The *Géode* does not admit children under age 3 or women late in pregnancy. The *Cinaxe* does not admit children under 4 and discourages pregnant women and heart and epilepsy patients from attending. If you want fare that's a bit tamer, the **Louis-Lumiére Cinema** offers 3D films throughout the day. The Planetarium features ever-changing shows about the stars and planets.

You can also borrow one of the City's 4,000 science videos to play in an on-site audio-visual facility, or try one of its 400 educational software programs on the spot. If you live nearby and become a subscriber, you can even take them home for three weeks—or some of its half-million books. The library even has an extensive collection of science and technology books in Braille.

There's more! Outside is the **Argonaute**, once an active submarine in the French Navy, now on permanent exhibition at the Cité des Sciences. Watch your head as you walk through!

The Argonaute is an authentic submarine you can walk through

The **Aquarium** displays more than 200 species of fish and gives a picture of what life is like at the bottom of the Mediterranean Sea.

Two special areas give young visitors careful attention. **Children's Cité** has separate 1½ -hour programs for children 3-5 and 6-12 on science related topics throughout the day. **Techno Cité** allows children 11 and older to try different sorts of technology from computer programing to flying a helicopter simulator. It's usually reserved for school groups, but is open to the public on Wednesday and Saturday afternoons and during school holidays.

Cité des Sciences et de l'Industrie, 30 Avenue Corentin-Cariou. Metro 7: Porte de la Villette. Closed Monday. Carte Musées. Admission covers the exhibition hall, submarine, planetarium, and some other attractions. Separate fees for the Géode, Cinaxe, and Children's Cité.

Vincennes

The Bois de Vincennes has everything you could want on a sunny outing: a medieval castle and chateau, a grand forest (no longer deep and dark. Quite a tame forest, really), a world-class zoo, beautiful parks and gardens, plenty of outdoor recreation, and, at the right time of the year, the largest fun fair (carnival) in France. Better yet, all this is just beyond the eastern edge of the Périphérique, minutes from the center of the city via Metro or RER. Put all those pieces together and you have much more than you can do in just one day. The forest is the largest in the region, with more than 150,000 trees and miles of paths and trails, perfect for running off pent-up energy or having a quiet Sunday afternoon picnic.

The bois offers ponds for boating, outdoor concerts, trails for bicycling and horseback riding and racing, a miniature railroad—even a Buddhist temple.

Chateau and Fortress

The donjon at Vincennes still looks unconquerable

When you emerge from the Metro, you're right in front of the entrance to the complex, a great fortress of the kings of France for 300 years. You first come to the **Tour du Village**, built in the 1660s as a governor's residence and now filled with period furniture and displays. Follow the promenade past the other seventeenth-century military buildings to the **donjon**, or keep, on your right. Newly restored, this castle is the oldest part of the complex, begun in 1337. More than 50 meters (170 feet) high, the keep has a fine spiral staircase leading you from floor to floor, up to the very battlements. You can look out from the windows here and experience the confident, impregnable feeling the king's soldiers must have had centuries ago. Kitchens were on the ground floor, a throne room on the first floor, and the royal household and bedchambers filled the top floor.

The **chapel** is also well preserved. Finished in the 1550s, it contains much of its original sixteenth-century stained glass. Spend some time walking through the grounds and looking out over the moat at the park beyond. It's a setting fit for a king, which indeed it was until the palace at Versailles was completed in the seventeenth century. Since the court moved, the chateau has had a rather mixed history. The castle was a state prison for more than a century. A porcelain factory was set up here for nearly 30 years; Napoléon refortified it as an important arsenal in the early nineteenth century.

Vincennes continued to serve as a key military outpost for more than another century. The spy Mata Hari was executed here in 1917, and it was a German military headquarters during the Occupation of World War II.

Chateau de Vincennes. Metro 1: Chateau de Vincennes; RER A: Vincennes. Carte Musées. Under 12 free.

Parc Floral

The beds of the Parc Floral de Paris, a huge flower park (30 hectares or 75 acres) are planted with such variety that they bloom continuously during the warm weather. Flower shows are held here in every season. Special areas include a physic garden for medicinal plants and herbs, a tropical garden, and a horticultural school. The Parc Floral is best reached from the same Metro station as the chateau.

Lac Daumesnil

This is the largest lake in the bois with pleasant islands in the middle for walking or picnicking. There's even a restaurant on Ile de Reuilly. There's a kiosk for renting bicycles and boats next to the lake, and a Buddhist temple sits near its shore.

> *Tip:* Lake Daumesnil, the zoo, and the fun fair are on the south side of the bois. You can certainly walk from the chateau, but if you're going for just these attractions, easiest access is Metro 8: Porte Dorée.

Parc Zoologique

This is the largest zoo in France, much more modern than the Ménagerie (Chapter 14), but less intimate. There are hundreds of species living here, the entire usual assortment of zoo creatures, but some less common ones, too, particularly the panda Yen-Yeb. In the center is a huge artificial rock over 60 meters high (more than 200 feet). You can actually go up inside the rock for close-up views of the mountain goats and wild sheep that live there.

Foire du Trône

If you're in Paris between Palm Sunday and the end of May, don't miss the largest carnival in France, the Foire du Trône. Packed with rides and games and lots of things to eat that are bad for you, the fair has roots that reach back more than a thousand years. It's held on the expansive lawn just south of Lac Daumesnil.

There's plenty more to keep everyone busy for a day in the bois, a nice day away from busy streets and traffic fumes. You'll find playgrounds, mini-golf, little cars to drive—all sorts of outdoor recreation. After an outing like this, everyone enjoys the more urban delights of the city with a renewed freshness and energy. No matter how fascinating the city, we've always found that we need a fix of trees at least once a week. This is a great place to get it.

Bois de Boulogne

The Bois de Boulogne is not quite as large as the Bois de Vincennes, but it's just as popular. This large park is just beyond the western edge of the city and just as accessible as Vincennes. Like its eastern mate, this bois is perfect for picnics, quiet (or noisy) walks, and general running around after days of being on one's best behavior in more public places. Here, too, there are lots of opportunities for recreation like biking and boules, horseback riding and skating. You can rent boats at **Lac**

Superieur (which, curiously, is both smaller and more southerly than Lac Inferieur). There's also a Shakespeare Garden, containing all the varieties of trees and plants mentioned in his plays, where open-air performances are given in the summer.

Jardin d'Acclimation

The best part of the bois— at least for younger kids—is the Jardin d'Acclimation, a terrific

---

Parc Yourself at La Villette

The Parc de la Villette is wonderful for picnics, and has a selection of restaurants throughout the facilities. You can stroll through the park, walk along the canal, and play among the bright red architectural follies that dot the landscape,

Also in the park is the Cité de la Musique, with displays of more than 900 types of musical instruments, as well as concert halls and demonstrations. The park offers sculpture classes, a terrific playground with an enormous dragon slide, and much more. A day out? Not early enough!

---

small-scale amusement park. While many of the attractions are geared for children younger than 10 or 12, there's plenty here to keep everyone in the family amused. There are lots of tame rides, a petting zoo, aviary, and little farm. You can watch puppet shows, laugh in the hall of mirrors, ride a pony, sail radio-controlled boats on the pond, or drive bumper cars. But even older kids might want to rent a bike and try the motocross course, drive the grand-prix style go-cart track, play mini-golf, video games or billiards, visit the popular culture museum, or try their hands at carnival games on the midway. There's even a resident circus.

It can be an expensive outing, but it's a place where you can spend a full day. Admission is about 13F per person—but each attraction costs extra. You can buy a carnet of sixteen tickets for about 150F, but some attractions take extra tickets or cash. It would be easy for a family to spend 500F here (€76 or $90) in an afternoon, not counting lunch and snacks. But you're welcome to bring a picnic and it's a *much* less expensive outing than the theme parks that close this chapter—and frankly, just as much fun. If your kids' ages span too wide a range, this might be another time to split up, with the older members of the clan finding their own amusement for the afternoon and the younger ones spending the day playing and laughing—like kids!

The Bois de Boulogne can be reached via several stations on Metro line 9 and Porte Dauphine in line 2, as well as several stations on RER C. If you enter the park at Porte Maillot, a miniature train will take you to the entrance of the Jardin d'Acclimation. Cost is about 25F, which includes entrance to the amusement park and the return train trip.

The Big Theme Parks

Paris is itself one of the world's greatest theme parks. You've got huge quantities of food, spectacular sights, even hair-raising rides—try a taxi through a tunnel or around Etoile! Why would you want to travel to an expensive theme park?

Frankly, that's not one of the recommendations in this book; Paris itself seems more than enough. But if you're in Paris for a lengthy visit and the kids insist, Mom and Dad might get their arms twisted into it. After a rough start, Disneyland Paris has established itself as a prime European tourist attraction, and **Parc Astérix** gives a very French spin to the amusement park business.

Disneyland Paris

If you've been to one of the Disney parks in the United States, you know just what to expect, except the park employees and costumed characters speak both French and English, and often other languages. (Look for the little flag badges they wear to tell what languages they speak.) You have your choice of dozens of admission and hotel plans that vary by hotel, by specific floor of the hotel, by time of the year, by day of the week, and probably by direction of the wind. You'll do better to stay in your Paris apartment, buy a 1-day pass, and take the RER to the park. One-day passes for a family of four during the summer will cost something over 700F.

No—Icky Mouse isn't the one you want...

There's no doubt that Disney knows how to keep everybody entertained. You'll have nonstop activity, except for standing in lines, and a mix of American and French popular culture, music, and breathless fun. Disney has even bent its corporate "no alcohol" policy to suit French taste—wine is now available in some restaurants. And there's more fun on the way: In 1999 the company announced that it would build an adjacent theme park offering visitors a behind-the-scenes look at movie-making, loaded with special effects, and similar to the Disney-MGM park in Florida. Opening is scheduled for 2002.

It's now possible to get to Disneyland Paris directly from the city center. RER A4 has been extended to the park. You can pick up the train at five central Paris stations but make sure you look at the destination on the front. Line A2 goes to Boissy-St-Léger. That's not the one you want.

Parc Astérix

To try a French approach to the theme park business instead of an American approach, consider Parc Astérix, based on the French cartoon character Astérix the Gaul and his sidekick Obelix. The park is built around the idea of time traveling through the history of France from the time of Gaul, to Greek and Roman periods, to the middle ages and up to the present time, with characters from each era.

Each era has its characteristic rides, like a water flume ride (with stones instead of logs) and the *Tonnerre de Zeus* (Zeus's Thunder), a kilometer-long wooden roller coaster.

Like Disneyland, Parc Astérix focuses on rides, themes, characters, and food with lots of performers and nonstop entertainment from bungee jumpers to special-effects shows. Prices are a bit lower than Disney's, but not a lot. Still, it's a full day's worth of activity for the price.

Parc Astérix is best accessed by taking RER B3 to Charles De Gaulle airport (Terminal 1) and taking the shuttle bus to the park. There is an additional charge for the bus.

Recommendations

✔ Get out of the urban center for some relaxed fun at least once if you're staying in Paris for more than a week.

✔ If anyone in your family is even the slightest bit interested in science, the Cité des Sciences is a must.

Part III
The Planning Pages

P art III will help you deal with the nuts-and-bolts issues of making this trip successful. Chapter 18 presents a catalog of all the attractions covered in this book, and puts them in an easy-to-use format for every member of your family to make selections about what to see. Chapter 19 lays out some possible itineraries for one- and two-week stays and shows you how to put together a well-paced visit to Paris. Chapter 20 will help you with your finances, providing forms for evaluating accommodations, for seeking inexpensive airfare, and for projecting your budget.

The idea behind *Paris for Families* is to make a holiday like this as easy and as stress-free as possible for your family. This section is designed to help you with that planning, leaving you nothing to worry about but getting postcards off to everyone on your list. Say—Don't forget to send one to *me*!

18. Top Attractions

W e've spent the last eight chapters going through the top family attractions in Paris. How do you choose? There's no way you can see all this in a week or two—or more!—and not emerge both crazy and unpopular. This is a vacation, not an endurance contest.

The easiest approach would probably be for Mom and Dad to sit down some evening and draw up an itinerary. The most efficient approach isn't always the best, though, and that's especially true in the case of a major family vacation. Remember what Chapter 9 recommended: Everyone needs to participate in deciding what to do... everybody who is old enough to know what's going on *needs* to be part of the planning. That way, *everybody* has a stake in the success of the trip.

Family trips can be more fun than anything you'll ever do, or they can be nightmares. The difference is usually the extent to which everybody is committed to making sure that everybody else has as good a time as they do. So it's important for everybody to talk about what they want and what they *don't* want.

Here's an approach that has always worked for the Lains. Maybe it's more complex than you need, but at least follow its spirit, even if you differ in the details. Before our trips, we'd read whatever we could get our hands on about our destination— that's everybody, not just Mom and Dad. We'd make a long list of things to do: attractions, experiences, walks... whatever we could think of.

Next, we'd talk about them. Dinnertime was always a good time for us, but so was driving somewhere in the car or lazing around on Sunday afternoon. All this talk had two important results. First, it got everybody excited about the trip, about all the fun we could have at our destination. Second, it got everyone thoroughly familiar with all the things there were to see and do.

Then we'd give everybody, parents included, a list of all the things we'd talked about and asked them to mark each one as
•something they *really* wanted to see or do;
•something that would be fun;
•something they had no real opinion about; or
•something they did *not* want to see or do.

We also asked everyone to list his or her top three things to see or do in order of importance.

When all the votes were tallied, we were able to sit down and rough out a list of things to do. But we kept two principles in mind. We gave more weight to the kids' choices than the parents'. This trip was mostly for them, after all. Barb and I knew we'd have chances to set our own agenda after they were grown. (We were right—we do.) Kids who have been an important part of the planning are going to be much more cheerful and tolerant than kids who have been consulted in just a token way. We also made sure that everybody, including parents, got his or her first choice, even if nobody else voted for it. Everyone agreed in advance to be tolerant of what others liked in exchange for everyone being tolerant of their choices. It always worked great.

Armed with that information, we were able to start to build a rough itinerary, balancing what we *wanted* to do with what was *possible* to do. It always involved some juggling, but we *always* honored our commitment to make sure everybody got his or her first choice.

If that's a more complicated system than you need, devise whatever will work for your family. But to make planning easier, the next few pages have a list you can use of all the attractions and experiences discussed in the book. You can make copies of these pages for voting, if you'd like, so each person has the complete list and can spend some time over it. (Or even better, buy each person his of her own copy of the book.... No? I didn't think you'd go for that.)

The list is arranged by the chapter of the main entry for each attraction, with other chapter numbers in parentheses in which an attraction is also discussed. Of course some of these things you'll see anyway, just in the normal course of walking around, but everything in the chapters is listed, in case you want to make a special point of getting somewhere.

Every family is different, of course, but attractions that hold wide appeal for almost all families are highlighted in bold. Now sharpen your pencil; Here's the list:

CHAPTER 10—MARVELOUS STRUCTURES
❑ **Arc de Triomphe** *[at Place Charles De Gaulle]*
❑ Assemblée Nationale
❑ Centre Georges-Pompidou *[Pompidou Center]* (also Ch. 13)
❑ Grand Palais (also Ch. 15)
❑ La Grande Arche *[at La Défense]*
❑ Hôtel de Ville *[city hall]*
❑ Institute du Monde Arabe *[Islamic Cultural Center]*
❑ La Madeleine (also Ch. 16)
❑ Musée des Plans-Reliefs *[relief maps & city models]*

❑ Palais de l'Élysée *[presidential mansion]*
❑ Palais Royal
❑ Petit Palais
❑ Pont Alexamdre III
❑ Pont Neuf
❑ **Tour Eiffel** *[Eiffel Tower]*

CHAPTER 11—GRAVES, GHOSTS, AND RUINS

❑ **Arènes de Lutèce** *[Roman arena]*
❑ **Catacombs**
❑ Cimetiere du Pére Lachaise *[cemetery]*
❑ Cimetiére de Montmartre
❑ Cimetiére du Montparnasse
❑ **Conciergerie**
❑ Crypte Archéologique *[crypt with Roman & Parisii ruins]*
❑ Les Egouts *[Sewer tour]*
❑ Mémorial de la Déportation *[monument to concentration camp deportees]*
❑ Mémorial du Martyr Juif Inconnu *[memorial to Jewish Holocaust victims]*
❑ Musée National du Moyen Age *[Cluny Museum of the Middle Ages]*
❑ Panthéon
❑ Place de la Concorde *[with Egyptian obelisk]*
❑ Square du Temple

CHAPTER 12—HOLY GROUND

❑ Basilique Saint-Denis
❑ **Église du Dôme** *[Napoléon's tomb in Dôme Church]*
❑ Mosquée de Paris *[chief Mosque in the city]*
❑ Musée de Notre-Dame
❑ **Notre Dame Cathedral and Towers**
❑ Sacré-Coeur *[Sacred Heart Basilica]*

❑ **Saint-Chapelle**
❑ St-Eustache
❑ St-Germain l'Auxerrois
❑ St-Germain-des-Pres
❑ Square du Jean XXIII

CHAPTER 13—THE ART OF PARIS
❑ **Espace Montmartre Salvador Dali**
❑ Musée d'Orsay
❑ **Musée du Louvre**
❑ Musée l'Orangerie des Tuileries
❑ Musée National d'Art Moderne *[at Pompidou Center]*
❑ Musée Picasso
❑ **Musée Rodin**
❑ original artwork from local painters

CHAPTER 14—PARKS AND DIVERSIONS
❑ Aquaboulevard
❑ Canal cruise
❑ Cinémathèque Française *[classic cinema]*
❑ Jardin des Plantes *[botanical gardens]*
    ❑ **Ménagerie** *[zoo]*
❑ Jardin des Tuileries
❑ Jardin du Luxembourg
❑ Marché aux Fleurs *[flower market]*
❑ Marché aux Oiseaux *[caged bird market]*
❑ Micromania Sega Center
❑ Musée National d'Histoire Naturelle *[Natural History Museum]*
    ❑ Galerie de Minéralogie *[rocks and minerals]*
    ❑ Galerie Entomologique *[insects]*
    ❑ Galerie Paléobotanique *[botany]*

❏ Galerie Paléontologique *[fossils]*
❏ **Grande Galerie de l'Évolution** *[human development]*
❏ Parc Monceau
❏ Place Douphine
❏ Quai de la Mégisserie *[for pet shops]*
❏ **Seine cruises** *[Bateaux-mouches, Bateaux Parisiens, Batobus]*
❏ Square du Vert-Galant

CHAPTER 15—MUSEUM POTPOURRI
❏ Musée Carnavalet *[history of Paris]*
❏ Musée de l'Armée *[military museum]*
❏ Musée de l'Homme *[anthropology]*
❏ Musée de la Contrafaçon *[counterfeit fashion]*
❏ Musée de la Curiosité *[magic]*
❏ Musée de la Legion d'Honneur *[military honors and chivalry]*
❏ Musée de la Marine *[naval and nautical]*
❏ Musée de la Monnaie *[coins and medals]*
❏ Musée de la Poupée *[doll museum]*
❏ Musée de la Préfecture de la Police *[local police and crime]*
❏ Musée Grévin *[wax museum]*
❏ Palais de la Découverte *[science demonstrations]*
❏ stamp market Sundays on Avenue du Marigny

CHAPTER 16—WALKING AND SHOPPING
❏ **Avenue des Champs-Élysées**
❏ Boulevard St-Germain and cafés
❏ Circuses
❏ Les Grands Boulevards & Shopping
    ❏ Galeries Lafayette
    ❏ Marks and Spencer
    ❏ La Madeleine and Fauchon
    ❏ The Passages

❏ Le Printemps
❏ **La Samaritaine and rooftop view**
❏ Forum des Halles
❏ **Ile St-Louis and Maison Berthillon**
❏ **Latin Quarter**
    ❏ La Sorbonne
    ❏ Rue de la Harpe & Rue de la Huchette
    ❏ Rue Mouffetard
❏ Marais
    ❏ **Place des Vosges**
    ❏ Rue des Rosiers
    ❏ Village St-Paul
❏ **Montmartre**
    ❏ Sacré-Coeur (also Ch. 11)
    ❏ Place du Tertre
    ❏ Windmills on Rue Lepic
❏ Tour Montparnasse

CHAPTER 17—DAYS OUT
❏ Bois de Boulogne
    ❏ Jardin d'Acclimation *[amusement park]*
❏ **Cité des Sciences et de l'Industrie**
    ❏ Argonaute
    ❏ Children's Cité and Techno Cité
    ❏ Cinaxe
    ❏ **Exhibitions and experiences**
    ❏ Géode
❏ Parc de la Villette
❏ Disneyland Paris
❏ Parc Astérix
❏ Vincennes
    ❏ Chateau and Fortress

❏ Parc Floral *[formal gardens]*
❏ Lac Daumesnil
❏ Parc Zoologique *[zoo]*
❏ Foire du Trône *[spring fun fair]*

OTHER THINGS TO SEE AND DO
❏ Go on the Lain Walking Tour of Central Paris (Ch. 6)
❏ Have a picnic in the park
❏ Stop for crêpes
❏ Take a scenic bus ride
❏ Try different sorts of restaurants
❏ Walk along the River Seine
❏ _____
❏ _____
❏ _____
❏ _____
❏ _____
❏ _____
❏ _____
❏ _____
❏ _____

19. Sample Itineraries

No two families are alike, so there's no one-size-fits-all approach to seeing Paris. The itineraries in this chapter aren't intended to set your agenda for you, just to show you *how* a trip like this can be structured and paced. The things your family will select will depend on the ages of the children, how much traveling you've done, how long you have, and the sorts of things you like.

Some families can't get enough of art, so they will hit every art museum in this book and go out searching for more. Some families have a member who is unable to walk long distances, so instead of exploring the neighborhoods of Paris on foot, they'll opt for activities that allow for more frequent opportunities to sit down. The point is, that's OK. You can't make a wrong choice. If you pick something that doesn't measure up to what you thought it would be, the next stop will undoubtedly be better.

Most of the time, it's best to try to avoid doing two similar things on the same day. Only De Vinci himself would try to see both the Louvre and the Orsay on the same day, and only the Pope would be able to muster appropriate levels of awe in both

Notre Dame and Saint Chapelle on the same day. Try to spend part of each day walking in a new area, and space the biggest attractions out through the trip.

This is a good time to remind you that if some of the kids are old enough, it can be more fun for everyone to split up occasionally. And planning some free time—a television evening or time relaxing in the park—is as important as visiting the Eiffel Tower; everybody needs time to relax and let their legs go limp once in awhile. It's best not to plan evening activities more than half the time. Give everyone a chance to recuperate.

The itineraries seldom specify a day of the week, but remember that most attractions are closed at least one day a week, so you'll have to work around that. It's also a good idea to make sure that everybody's first-choice activity gets done early in the trip so no one has to be disappointed if there has to be a change of plans later.

There's no possible way you can see all of Paris in a week or two; you'll leave with more things you want to do than you had when you arrived. But maybe, just maybe, this is only your first family trip to Paris.

One-Week Itinerary

Arrival Day—If you've flown from overseas, follow the suggestions in Chapter 4 on moving in, napping, exploring, shopping and eating. By the time you finish the list, it should be late afternoon or early evening. If you'd like to get out, try a walk along the Seine. Go to the part of the river nearest your apartment or hotel, near Notre Dame if you're living east or near the Eiffel Tower if you're living west. Either way you'll see what you've come to Paris for. Finish the evening with a boat trip on the Seine, gazing at the illuminated monuments all along the river. Get to bed early tonight... *or*

...If you arrived by auto or train, you're not quite so tired.

Drivers should arrive in the late morning or early afternoon to avoid the worst traffic. After you get moved in to your apartment or hotel, you can start your sightseeing. You might begin in the heart of Paris, the Ile de la Cité. The view from the Square du Vert-Galant is a marvelous introduction to the city. You could visit the Conciergerie and Saint-Chapelle this afternoon, then stop for ice cream at Berthillon. Cross over to the Latin Quarter and explore some of the streets north of Boulevard St-Germain, and find a nice restaurant, perhaps on the Rue de la Harpe, for dinner. Afterwards, take a boat tour if it's not too late.

Day 2—Isn't it great to wake up in Paris! Hard to believe we're really here, after all the planning! Today let's fix breakfast, then see the highlights by taking the Lain Walking Tour from Chapter 6. We'll take the Metro to Cité and start at Notre Dame. You should have decided by now what the most efficient and economical way will be for using the Metro: carnet, Carte Orange, or Mobilis pass.

It's hard to resist peaking into places like Notre Dame as you pass. It's OK. You're on vacation—do what you want. But we'll make a longer visit later in the week. Depending on how fast you walk, you might be ready for lunch about the time you reach the Jardin des Tuileries, and there are snack bars there. Eat a baguette sandwich and watch kids sail boats in the pond. Maybe yours will join them!

If you have sturdy legs, you'll arrive at the Eiffel Tower about mid-afternoon. Since you've been walking, you probably won't want to walk up, but you should certainly take the elevator to the second or (Sure—go for it!) the third level. The kids will love picking out the route you've walked so far today. You'll have to stand in line for a while, but this is a great chance to snack on ice cream or crêpes. Take turns standing in line while the others gawk at the Tower or river, or just rest their feet on a bench.

When you come down from the Eiffel Tower, you can finish the walk (on foot or by bus) or save the rest for another day. Or, since you're in the neighborhood, you might go back to Invalides to see Napoléon's tomb or the Musée Rodin. Whatever you choose, you've worked up an appetite, so enjoy your supper tonight.

This evening, you might let your weary feet rest. Spend the evening in front of the TV or take that evening cruise on the Seine if you didn't do it last night.

Day 3—If you didn't visit Notre Dame yesterday at the beginning of your walk, start there today. Walk through the ancient church, and then climb the Towers for a stunning view of the Seine, the Latin Quarter, and the Marais. Afterwards, unless you've already covered the Latin Quarter thoroughly on your first day, this might be a good place to go. Just cross the Seine at the bridge near Notre Dame. (Or the one in the middle if the Ile St-Louis, if you're stopping for ice cream at Maison Berthillon.) If the Musée Cluny appeals to your family history buffs, spend an hour there. Perhaps you'd prefer the Panthéon. In any case, wander around the streets of the quarter, working your way slowly east so you can get a late lunch along Rue Mouffetard, visit the Arènes de Lutèce, and finish at the Jardin des Plantes, in the Grande Galerie de l'Évolution or the Ménagerie, or just trying the labyrinth in the park.

Tonight, if the weather is clear, you might go back to the Eiffel Tower for an unforgettable nighttime view over Paris. If it's rainy or misty, though, save it for another night.

Day 4—Let's devote this morning to art. We'll have to choose either the Louvre or the Orsay; there's just not time to do both. Drat! We'll just have to make another trip to Paris *next* year. At the Louvre, you'll want to see the famous *Mona Lisa* and the disarmingly beautiful *Venus de Milo* as well as all the famous works you can squeeze into a couple of hours. Or you might choose to wander amid the famous Impressionist works at the Orsay for the same time.

Afterwards, a nice change of pace would be to go to the Place des Vosges area for lunch. From the Louvre, take the Metro (Line 1) from the Musée du Louvre station four stops to St-Paul, just a short walk from the square. From the Orsay, take the Metro (Line 12) from the Solférino station two stops to Concorde, change to Line 1, and go six stops to St-Paul.

At Place des Vosges you'll find plenty of cafés to choose from, or lots of places to buy picnic items to eat in the park while you take off your shoes and relax. After lunch, you might split up for awhile, with different groups visiting some of the museums they'd most like to see in the area, doing some shopping, or just exploring on their own. This is a great area for all three. Free time is important, and this is a good day for it.

Meet back at the park later, or at the apartment for dinner. This might be a good evening just to relax and recharge your batteries.

Day 5—If you're flying back the day after tomorrow, remember to call your airline to reconfirm your reservations this morning.

If this is a Saturday or Sunday morning, the Catacombs open at 9. This is a great time to go if anyone is interested. Anybody who doesn't care to do that can go out to Parc de la Villette and the Cité des Sciences. [Catacomb visitors can go out there, too, after they finish with the bones. Just take the Metro at Denfert Rochereau (Line 6) four stops to Place d'Italie and change to Line 7. Take that all the way to Porte de la Villette. It looks like a long way, but it takes only 20 minutes. You can arrange to meet at noon outside near the Géode or inside under the spaceman.]

The Cité des Sciences will occupy as much time as you care to spend. There's plenty to do in and around the museum and park. When you finish, you can walk along the canal or take a ride on one of the boats back into central Paris. Or, if it's Tuesday through Friday, you can visit the Catacombs from 2 to 4 in the afternoon if you like, and finish the day relaxing at a puppet show in nearby Luxembourg Gardens.

If the kids are too small to be interested in science (although there's a lot for all ages at La Villette), a day tromping in the Bois de Boulogne and playing in the Jardin d'Acclimation might be a great choice.

Tonight might be a nice evening to just hop on a bus and ride for an hour, looking at parts of Paris you haven't seen, or for walking along the quais or boulevards.

Day 6—This is awful! Today's our last day in Paris and we haven't *begun* to see everything we want! Where did the time go? Well, there's still time to get to a couple of other places we really want to see. After breakfast, it's off to Montmartre to see Sacré-Coeur, windmills, streets only a mountain goat would appreciate, and the Salvador Dali museum, and to do some shopping. Then we can take the Metro (Line 12) from Abbesses to Concorde and stroll up the Champs-Élysées. You'll find plenty of places to shop (lots of expensive stores and some great arcades) and eat (Magic Burger XXL, anyone?) and by evening we'll be at the Arc de Triomphe, with plenty of time to climb to the top for a last birds-eye view of Paris.

Now, at the end of the stay, treat yourself to dinner in a nice restaurant, then go back to your apartment or hotel and pack. But before bedtime, just slip back down to the river again, if you can, for a last stroll in this magical city.

Day 7—You might not have much time today. If you're flying, you need to be at the airport well before your departure. If you're driving or taking the train home, you might have time to visit another museum or two, but even if you can, so much is left undone! But it was a fabulous vacation, everybody had a terrific time, and you're probably already thinking about coming back another time. *Bon voyage!*

Two-Week Itinerary

The great thing about spending two weeks in Paris is that you don't have to rush as much. You can take more time to explore neighborhoods, visit small museums, and go back to somewhere you really liked. You can try more different places to eat and even sleep late once in awhile. You can have even more of a sense of Living Like a Local. The days in this section aren't packed quite as full as days in the one-week itinerary, so you'll have more time to wander, to sit at a sidewalk table and sip hot chocolate, to pursue special interests from other parts of this book.

This section doesn't include day-by-day evening activities as the previous section did, but lists possibilities at the end. It's still a good idea, even with a two-week trip's more leisurely pace, to spend no more than half your evenings doing something. Everyone will be more rested and cheerful if they have several evenings just to relax, to read, or to watch TV.

Day 1—Same as in one-week itinerary. You might make your first sightseeing stop at Notre Dame. Climbing the towers won't raise blisters like too much walking will, and you *will* get some circulation back in your legs after your travels!

Day 2—Same as in one-week itinerary.

Day 3—There's so much to see and do in the Latin Quarter that it's worth a whole day. This way you can visit the Cluny *and* the Panthéon, have mock gladiatorial combat in the arena, munch your way down Rue Mouffetard, and loll around in the Jardin des Plantes. Or pick some of the other attractions you'd like to visit in the Quarter—the police museum, the Institute de

Monde Arabe, the Mosquée de Paris, the Ménagerie, some of the units of the Natural History Museum. Tonight have dinner at a restaurant in the Quarter. Keep your eye on the menus in front as you stroll today.

Day 4—You might go back to the Invalides Quarter today. Try the sewer tour, if you're inclined. Visit the Musée Rodin, Napoléon's tomb and, if you like, the Musée de l'Armée. Then stroll across the Champ de Mars, under the Eiffel Tower, and cross the river. Try one or two of the museums in the Palais de Chaillot, if that's appealing, or walk through the upscale 16th Arrondissement to the Musée de la Contrafaçon. This might be a good afternoon to split up, if people have different interests, or for older kids to set off on their own.

Day 5—How about going to the Louvre today? You can spend a couple of hours there this morning, lunch in the Tuileries, stop by La Samaritaine for the rooftop view, and stroll over to Les Halles to do a little shopping. Don't forget to stop at St. Eustache for a picture with the sculpture of the giant head and hand!

Day 6—This might be a good time for a day-long expedition to the Parc de la Villette and Cité des Sciences described in the one-week itinerary, finishing up with a stroll or ride along the Canal St-Martin.

Day 7—You might spend today in the Marais. Start from the Hôtel de Ville, walk up to the Pompidou Center and try the modern art museum. Or wander through the shops in the Village St-Paul and check out the Musée Picasso or Musée Carnavalet. There are other places to see, as well, museums of dolls or magic, interesting streets in the Jewish Quarter, and places to relax like the Place des Vosges or Square du Temple. If anyone would like to try the Cimetiere du Pére Lachaise, it's not far away—take

Metro Line 3 from Temple. This is another day when people might like to go separate directions, but it would also be ideal for just relaxing in a park for a couple of hours together.

Day 8—Start today at Place de la Concorde and stroll up the Avenue des Champs-Élysées. Take your time and turn aside as it pleases you. There are science and art exhibits to see at the Grand Palais and Petit Palais, and much else along the way. Eventually you'll reach the Arc de Triomphe and will get another of those fabulous aerial views of the city. From here, you might like to go on the Metro (Line 1) or RER (Line A) and see La Grande Arche at La Defense, and all the modern architecture in that area. It's a remarkable place.

Day 9—Get back to Paris's roots today. We haven't really explored the islands, so let's start on the Ile de la Cité. You've already seen Notre Dame, but Saint Chapelle is breathtaking. The Conciergerie is interesting and spooky; places like the Square du Vert-Galant and Place Dauphine are picturesque and peaceful. Try the Crypte Archéologique in the plaza in front of Notre Dame and the peaceful Square du Jean XXIII behind. Then cross to the Ile St-Louis and stroll along the peaceful old streets, not forgetting to stop for ice cream at Berthillon. This is a day with a lot to see in a fairly small area.

Day 10—If you'd like to see Paris at its most charming, you might spend some time today in that village within the city, Montmartre. Look out over the city from the plaza in front of Sacré-Coeur, and tour the cavernous church. Watch the artists in Place du Tertre, see the Dali museum, puff your way up steep stepped streets, find the windmills on Rue Lepic. You'll find comfortable cafés and bistros galore here on the roof of Paris, and attractive streets and squares. If you'd like something different this afternoon you might take Metro Line 13 from

Place de Clichy to Basillique de Saint-Denis, burial place of the kings of France, or Line 12 from Abbesses to Montparnasse on the south side of Paris and look out over the city from Tour Montparnasse.

Day 11—It should be time for another all-day excursion. There are several good choices, but if it's a nice day, I might pick Vincennes. The chateau and castle will hold everyone's interest, but later you can take your picnic lunch and sit by the lake. Afterwards go boating on the lake and spend some time at the zoo. There are paths to hike, playgrounds to romp in, and formal gardens to admire. Or, maybe best of all, take books to read, postcards to finish, travel journals to write in, and just spend the day relaxing and enjoying each others' company. If you'd rather, the Bois de Boulogne is also tailor-made for a family outing. Centerpiece is the amusement park, the Jardin d'Acclimation—enough games and rides for a busy day. But there is also a museum of popular arts, an herb garden, and lots of outdoor activities.

Day 12—If you've got an international flight home in a couple of days, telephone the airline to reconfirm your reservations this morning. Then maybe it's time for another dose of art. Spending the morning among the Impressionists at the Orsay is wonderful, although the Orangerie in the Jardin des Tuileries is also a tempting possibility. Both places are filled with vivid, colorful painting; you'll recognize something on every wall. Afterwards, a walk east along the Left Bank of the Seine will take you to the bustling area around St-Germain-des-Pres. This area is fun to wander. It's filled with galleries, cafés, restaurants, shops, crowds, markets, street entertainers—one of the busiest and most engaging areas of Paris. You might elect to spend the rest of the day here, settling, finally, on a nice restaurant for a leisurely dinner. Agree on a time and place to meet if some of your group plans to strike off on their own for a while.

Day 13—How can this be our last day in Paris? Didn't we just get here? Maybe we should do a little bit of serious shopping today. The Opera Quarter and Les Grands Boulevards are home to the great department stores like Le Printemps and Galeries Lafayette, as well as many of the arcaded Passages that are filled with fascinating shops and boutiques. La Madeleine and Fauchon are nearby. If some of your group really don't see the fun in shopping, you're also near the Hard Rock Café, the wax figures at Musée Gréven, and the Micromania Sega Center. But all good things must end. Eventually you'll need to take your purchases and memories back to your apartment or hotel and pack them away for the trip home. If you've spent two weeks in Paris, it will be hard to leave. You've been living like a local and feel a real connection to the place. Can you be homesick for a place you've only lived in for two weeks? You bet! You'll find out once you've been back home for a few months. Over dinner one night, somebody will start reminiscing about something you saw together in Paris, and suddenly the table will get quiet. Everybody is wishing they could go back and do it again. You've got a new bond, one that will last forever.

Paris Nights

You shouldn't schedule activities every night. You need time to catch your breath. On our trips, about half the time in the evenings we've played games, watched television, or just sprawled on the floor with a book, just like at home. If we go out in Paris, having dinner at a restaurant, with its slow Parisian pace, might keep us occupied until bedtime. Other evening activities are apt to be those that let us wind down from a busy day.

If you're spending your days in museums and galleries, spend several evenings just walking some of the Paris neighborhoods we've suggested in this book. Because the city is old and was built over time, there is a wonderful variety of streets and squares to wander. My own favorites are the Latin Quarter, St-Germain, and Montmartre.

Don't miss an after-dark cruise on the Seine. The buildings are illuminated all along the river and a nighttime cruise is spectacular and unforgettable.

The view from the Eiffel Tower at night is enough to give you chills. It's worth going to the top of the tower twice: once in daylight and once at night. They are very different experiences and I honestly can't say which one is better.

The Lains are always drawn to rivers, and a walk along the Seine at night is something it's impossible to get enough of.

Look at the bus map your *Petit Plan* and go for a ride. In the summer it stays light until quite late, so you can sightsee in neighborhoods without walking through them. You might just find somewhere you want to return to on foot another day for a better look.

Reality creeps in. If you're staying for more than a week or so, you might want to take one evening to do some laundry and go to the store and replenish your food supply.

And there are always parks. When the weather is nice, we do a lot of our relaxing outdoors, sometimes by taking a simple picnic supper (bread, cheese, beverages, and something sweet from the local bakery for dessert), and sometimes just taking something to read. This is less practical in the wintertime, it's true, but otherwise, it's a great way to end the day.

Paris in the Rain

Weather will be a problem only if you let it be. If you have outdoor activities planned for the day but it rains, switch to some indoor attractions—you will find no shortage of museums and galleries in Paris! Frankly, though, I've walked through a lot of cities in a lot of strange weather, and if you're going to walk in the rain *anywhere*, it doesn't get much better than Paris! When you walk through Paris in a mist, you have this eerie sense of having fallen into an Impressionist painting. Familiar landmarks reflect off the pavement, their light fractured and scattered by the droplets of water. Colors are softened and diffused here, vibrant and sharp there. Yes, a rainstorm will very likely interfere with your picnic, but if you've got your attitude on straight, it might make the neighborhood walk you'd planned even more memorable.

Paris in any weather—heat, cold, sun, rain, snow—is worth having. A vacation is never ruined by weather, only by your expectations of what the weather *ought* to be. (I will now get letters from a hundred people who have been in Paris during a 25-day monsoon, saying I'm wrong. OK. Monsoons of more than ten days are the exception to my assertion.) Live like a local: Take Paris on its own terms—and Enjoy!

20. Budget Worksheets

This chapter will provide several easy-to-use forms that you can use to plan your Paris holiday. First are two forms—even printed in French versions—for you to gather information about hotels and apartments, and to compare them easily. You can use them, too, for mail and fax contact, in case the proprietor speaks only French—and you don't. All the tips and techniques from Chapter 2 are included on the forms.

Next, for readers who will be flying to Paris, is a form you can fill out before you begin speaking to airlines and travel agents. This form, based on the advice in Chapter 3, can help you get the best airfare by outlining your travel requirements so you or your agent can be as flexible as possible.

Finally, the chapter contains a simple budget-planning form you can use to project your expenses, drawing from the suggestions you'll find throughout the book. This budget (like the usual Lain travel budgets) will probably estimate on the high side. It's always been our preference to have money left over rather than to run out before the end. We're pretty conservative financially.

Accommodations Forms

Apartments are ideal if you're staying in Paris for a week or more; they're far more home-like than any hotel room. Apartments are normally more economical than hotels and, because they're roomier, much more comfortable. You can also save money by cooking some of your own meals instead of having to eat every meal at a café or restaurant. But for stays of less than a week, it's harder to find an inexpensive apartment, so a large hotel room or suite, or two adjacent rooms, might be more economical. Always talk or write directly to the manager to get the best information and the best price.

Prices will usually be quoted in francs or euros. Convert these to your own currency by multiplying the amount by the exchange rate. In this book, for instance, we convert francs to U.S. dollars by multiplying by 0.182 (an exchange rate of $1 = 5.5F, a typical rate when *Paris for Families* went to press).

Once you've compiled a list of several possible apartments or hotels from the booklet from the Paris Office de Tourisme, or from some of the websites listed in the last section of this book, you're ready to begin making contact. Telephoning is the best way to gather basic information, with a follow-up letter or fax to the manager of the place you select. But it's easy to make arrangements by letter or fax, too. The forms in this section—in your own language or in French—can be used over the phone or in writing. Don't forget the free language translation website in Chapter 2; use it to compose your own letters or to translate replies from apartment and hotel managers.

Form 1a—Finding an apartment

1. Hello. I am looking for an apartment in Paris for ___ people. We will arrive on this date, _____ and will leave on _____, a total of ___ nights. There will be ___adults and ___children whose ages are _____.

2. We would like a...
   - ❏ studio apartment
   - ❏ 1-bedroom apartment
   - ❏ 2-bedroom apartment

Please describe the apartment, the building, and the neighborhood below:

3. What is the address of the apartment? What is the nearest Metro?
4. How large is the apartment? What floor is it on? How many beds?
5. What kind of bath/toilet facilities are in the apartment?
6. Does the apartment face the street or a courtyard? How quiet is it?
7. Describe the furnishings and appliances in the apartment. Is there a telephone? a television?
8. Describe the cooking facilities in the apartment. How much storage space is there?
9. Does the apartment have laundry facilities?
10. Describe the building. When was it last refurbished? Is there an elevator?
11. Describe the neighborhood. Is it residential, commercial, industrial?
12. How far away is the nearest self-service laundry? Grocery store? Bakery? Produce market?
13. How do we pick up the keys?
14. What is the best price you can give me, including all taxes?
15. Is there any way to reduce it further? (like length of stay, weekend specials, bringing our own linens for extra cots, etc.)
16. Do you accept credit cards or must we pay cash?

Thank you. If we decide to rent this apartment, I will confirm this with you within two weeks.

Paris for Families

French version—Form 1a

1. Bonjour. Je cherche un appartement à Paris pour ___ personnes. Nous arriverons le _____ [day first, then month] et partirons le _____, pour un total de _____ nuits . Il y aura _____ adultes et _____ enfants dont les âges sont _____.
2. Nous voudrions un ....

❏ studio ❏ appartement avec une chambre à coucher
❏ appartement avec deux chambres à coucher

Veuillez décrire l'appartement, le bâtiment, et le voisinage selon les questions suivantes:

3. Quelle est l'adresse de l'appartement? Quel est le Métro le plus proche?
4. De quelle grandeur est l'appartement? À quel étage? Combien de lits y a-t-il?
5. Qu'est-ce qu'il y a comme bain/douche/w.c. dans l'appartement?
6. L'appartement donne-t-il sur la rue ou sur la cour? Est-il tranquille ou bruyant?
7. Décrivez les meubles et les appareils ménagérs dans l'appartement. Y a-t-il un téléphone? une télévision?
8. Comment l'appartement est-il équipé pour faire la cuisine? Quelle sorte de placards ou d'espace de rangement y a-t-il?
9. Y a-t-il une machine à laver ou un séchoir dans l'appartement?
10. Décrivez le bâtiment. Quand a-t-il été rénové la dernière fois? Y a-t-il un ascenseur?
11. Décrivez le voisinage. Est-il résidentiel, commercial, industriel?
12. À quelle distance est la laverie automatique la plus proche? L'épicerie? La boulangerie? Le marché?
13. Comment prendrons-nous les clés?
14. Quel est le meilleur prix que vous pouvez me donner, toutes taxes comprises?
15. Y aurait-il d'autres réductions possibles (par exemple pour les séjours de longue durée, un forfait weekend? les draps fournis par les clients pour les lits supplémentaires , etc...)
16. Prenez-vous des cartes de crédit ou devons-nous payer en argent comptant?

Merci. Si nous décidons de louer cet appartement, je vous confirmerai ceci dans un délai de deux semaines.

Form 1b—Finding a hotel

1. Hello. I am looking for a hotel in Paris for ___ people. We will arrive on this date, _____ and will leave on _____, a total of ___ nights. There will be ___adults and ___children whose ages are _____.
2. Where is the hotel? What's the nearest Metro?
3. How large is the room?
4. What kind of bath/toilet facilities are in the room? Do you have less expensive rooms with share toilet facilities?
5. What is the charge for extra people?
6. Are rollaway beds available for extra people?
7. If we don't use a rollaway or bring our own linens for it, is there a deduction? How much?
8. Does the room face the street or a courtyard? How quiet is it? Is there an elevator?
9. Does the room have a telephone? Television? Alarm clock? Coffee maker? Hair drier?
10. Is breakfast provided? What does it consist of?
11. If we don't take breakfast, how much will you deduct from our rate?
12. How far away is the nearest self-service laundry?
13. What is the best price you can give me, including all taxes?
14. Is there any way to reduce it further? (like length of stay, weekend specials, etc.)
15. Do you have suites available? What is the price? Please describe them.
16. Could we get two adjacent rooms? At what price? How much money would we save if one of the rooms did not have toilet facilities?
17. Do you accept credit cards or must we pay cash?

Thank you. If we decide to rent this room, I will confirm this with you within two weeks.

French version—Form 1b

1. Bonjour. Je recherche un hôtel à Paris pour _____ personnes. Nous arriverons le _____ [day, then month] et partirons le _____, pour un total de ___ nuits. Il y aura ___adultes et ____ enfants dont les âges sont _____.

2. Où est l'hôtel? Quel est le Métro le plus proche?
3. De quelle grandeur est la chambre?
4. Qu'est-ce qu'il y a comme bain, douche, ou w.c. dans la chambre? Avez-vous des chambres moins chères avec les w.c. sur l'étage?
5. Quel est le prix pour les personnes supplémentaires?
6. Est-ce que des lits pliants sont disponibles pour les personnes supplémentaires?
7. Si nous n'utilisons pas un lit pliant qui est dans la chambre, ou si nous apportons nos propres draps pour le lit pliant, est-ce qu'il y a une réduction? Combien?
8. La chambre donne-t-elle sur la rue ou sur la cour? Est-ce qu'elle est bruyante ou tranquille? Est-ce qu'il y a un ascenseur?
9. La chambre a-t-elle un téléphone? Une télévision? Un réveil-matin? Une machine à café? Un sèche-cheveux?
10. Le petit déjeuner est-il fourni? En quoi consiste-il?
11. Si nous ne prenons pas le petit déjeuner, combien déduirez-vous de notre note?
12. À quelle distance la laverie automatique la plus proche est-elle?
13. Quel est le meilleur prix que vous pouvez me donner, toutes taxes comprises?
14. Y a –t-il d'autres réductions possibles (par exemple pour les séjours de plus longue durée, un forfait week-end, etc.)
15. Avez-vous des appartements ou suites disponibles? À quel prix? Pourriez-vous les décrire?
16. Pourrions-nous obtenir deux chambres contiguës? À quel prix? Combien d'argent économiserions-nous si une des chambres n'avait pas de w.c.?
17. Prenez-vous des cartes de crédit ou devons-nous payer en argent comptant?

Merci. Si nous décidons de louer cette chambre, je vous confirmerai la réservation dans un délai de deux semaines.

Once you've gathered information about three or four apartments or hotels, you ought to be able to make a wise and informed choice about where to stay. Contact the manager again and make the booking, and follow up in writing with a letter or fax.

Finding the Best Airfare

Answer these questions for your travel agent or before you sit down to check websites and airlines. They'll help you get the best deal.

Form 2—Air travel requirements

1. How many people traveling? _____
   _____Adults_____Children under 18 (ages:_____)
   _____How many students?
   Depending on the route and the time of year, discounts may be available to students or children under certain a age.

2. Departure date: _____
   Is this date ❑Fixed or is it ❑Flexible?
   If you can travel during Low or Shoulder season, airfares may be half or less of High Season (summer months) fares. Avoid Friday, Saturday, Sunday departures.

3. Length of stay? _____days/weeks
   Stays of 7 to 30 days usually qualify for the cheapest rates because business travelers usually stay for less than a week. Avoid return flights on Friday, Saturday, Sunday for better rates.

4. Preferred airline, if any?_____
   If you or another family member works for an airline, you may be eligible for deep discounts. Do you have a frequent flier account with an airline? If so, foreign travel can add considerable

mileage. Do you have enough miles in an account to get one or more tickets free?

5. Preferred airport, if any?_____
   You might save money by driving to a more distant airport where cheaper fares are offered. Price flights from all nearby airports.

6. Non-stop flight required or connection OK?
   ❑Non-stop only; ❑connection OK
   Unless you live near a city with non-stop service, this isn't an issue: you'll have to connect. But if there's a choice, the connection might be cheaper. If you have a choice of connecting cities, consider scheduling your flights to give yourself time for an excursion into the most interesting city. Make sure easy public transportation is available from the airport to city center.

7. Stopover en-route OK?
   ❑Yes; ❑No
   A few foreign carriers offer deep discounts to travelers willing to stay overnight in their countries, but accommodations and extra meals can eat away savings on airfare.

8. Check foreign carriers.
   Many carriers will make a stop in Paris on their way to other destinations in Europe, Africa, or Asia. You might find a bargain on something like Air India or Swissair.

9. Check consolidators.
   Some companies buy blocks of tickets from airlines and resell them at a discount. These can be great value, but check companies carefully: some very low advertised prices are scams. Travel agents may know who are the most reputable consolidators.

Armed with this information and these tips, you should be able to find the best fares available. Don't stop watching for sales after you buy your tickets, either. Airlines will often reissue more expensive tickets at sale prices for a service charge.

Your Holiday Budget

Here's your own personal bottom line: what it's going to take to give your family the vacation of a lifetime. The form is deliberately set up to estimate on the high side, but it's a wonderful feeling to come home from a great trip with money left over. Prices are given in francs and euros, and were current at the time of publication. Check the *Paris for Families* Web page for updated information.

Form 3—Your travel budget

_____1. Travel expenses
    Airfare, train tickets, or driving expenses, including meals during layovers or on the train or road, and overnight accommodation if you're driving a long distance.

_____2. Accommodation in Paris
    From Form Ia or Ib. If you're driving, include the cost of parking your car in this category.

_____3. Food: meals and snacks
    ■ *If you're staying in a hotel, you'll probably eat two or three meals per day in cafés and restaurants. If that's the case, allow 150F to 250F (23F-38F) per person, per day for meals, depending on the ages of your children.*
    ■ *If you're renting an apartment and plan to fix*

*breakfast and supper at home most of the time,
eating only lunch out, figure 80F to 150F (€12-
€23) per person, per day, a figure which also takes
the purchase of groceries into account. It's possible
to spend much more, of course, but these figures will
provide for you comfortably.*

*Per person/per day ___x number of days ____x
number in family =_____F/€*

4. Attractions and sightseeing
   *There are many free attractions, and the kids get in
   free to many places that cost their parents. You'll
   probably spend less than this but let's figure an
   average of 60F (€9) per person per day.*
   60F/€9 x ____people x ____days =_____F/€

5. Shopping and souvenirs
   *This is a very personal category. We suggest you
   give each child a fixed amount, perhaps 150F to
   300F (€22-€45), or a sum of perhaps 30F to 50F
   (€4.5-€8) per day to pay for souvenirs, snacks,
   etc. They can, of course, supplement that with
   their own money if they wish. Mom and Dad can
   set their own budget in this category. However, it
   is best to set a fixed amount in advance. Give the
   money to your children in francs when you
   arrive, perhaps a little at a time for younger ones.*

6. Local Transportation
   ■ *The Metro: This depends on whether you use
   a weekly Metro pass, whether your kids are
   young enough to qualify for discounts, and how
   much walking you like to do. But an average of
   20F (€3) should cover it.*

20F/€3 x ___ people x ___ days = _____ F/C

■ *Airport Transportation: If you fly into Paris, you'll probably take the RER or a bus into central Paris. Cost will be about 50F (€7.6) each way, but some of your children might be eligible for discounts.*
100F (€15) x ___people = _____ F/C

■ *Taxi: You might take a taxi to your hotel or apartment from the RER station, or have occasion to use one during your visit. Let's budget <u>200F (€30).</u>*

Total Expenses in Categories 1 through 6 above _____

That's your budget. Convert everything to your own currency, because you can't compare apples to eggplants and come out with a meaningful number. For example, if you've used francs in categories 2 through 6 and want to convert the number to U.S. dollars, multiply by 0.182 (or the current exchange rate). To be on the safe side we usually add a contingency fund of about 10% of the total. We've never needed it, but it's nice to have a cushion.

Appendix

Words to Know

This list is not intended to be a comprehensive dictionary, but to present some of the words you are likely to see in print—timetables, opening hours, street and directional signs. An inexpensive dictionary and/or phrase book will help you communicate verbally more than this list is intended to. Many of those sorts of books have specialized dictionaries of restaurant menu items, medical terminology, and so on. The words here are those you are most likely to want to *read* in order to find your way or get basic information.

Many words may be preceded by *la* or *le* (the feminine and masculine articles) or with *l'* if the word begins with a vowel sound. (Examples: *la gare, le jardin, l'addition*). Some listed words may end with an *e* not shown below, depending on gender in the context.

à bientôt	see you soon
accès interdit	do not enter
addition	restaurant bill or check
alimentation	grocery store
an	year
appartement	apartment
après	after
après-midi	afternoon
arrêt	stop
ascenseur	elevator, lift
au revoir	goodbye
autoroute	highway, motorway

avant	before
banque	bank
bateau	boat
bière	beer
bienvenu	welcome
billets	tickets
bois	forest
boisson	beverage
bonjour	hello, good day
bonne nuit	good night
bonsoir	good evening
boulangerie	bakery
cabine téléphonique	phone booth
café	café, black coffee
caisse	cashier
chambre	bedroom or room
charcuterie	delicatessen
chaud	hot
complet	full, fully booked
correspondance	transfer, connection
dames	ladies' room
déjeuner	lunch
dîner	supper
direction	destination
douche	shower
eau	water
école	school
église	church
enfant	child
entrée	entrance, way in or appetizer, starter
escalier	stairs
essence	gasoline, petrol
étage	floor (2ème étage = 2nd floor)
étudiant	student

femme	woman
fermé	closed
froid	cold
fumeurs	smoking
gare	railway station
glace	ice cream, ice
guichet	ticket office
heure	hour
heures d'ouverture	opening hours
hommes	men, men's room
interdit	not allowed, forbidden
jardin	garden
jour	day
laverie	self-serve launderette
libre	free
ligne	line
marché	market
matin	morning
merci	thank you
messieurs	gentlemen, men's room
midi	noon
non potable	not drinkable
non	no
non-fumeure	no smoking
nuit	night
occupé	occupied
oui	yes
ouvert	open
pain	bread
petit déjeuner	breakfast
porte	gate, door
potable	drinkable
poussez	push
premiers secours	first aid

privé	private
s'il vous plâit	please
secours	help
soir	evening
sortie de secours	emergency exit
sortie	exit, way out
tabac	tobacconist
tarif réduit	reduced price
télécarte	phone card
timbres	postage stamps
tirez	pull
toilettes	toilets, rest rooms
traiteur	deli, carryout or takeaway shop
vin blanc	white wine
vin rouge	red wine

Days of Week

lundi	Monday
mardi	Tuesday
mercredi	Wednesday
jeudi	Thursday
vendredi	Friday
samedi	Saturday
dimanche	Sunday

Months of Year

janvier	January
février	February
mars	March
avril	April
mai	May
juin	June

juillet	July
août	August
septembre	September
octobre	October
novembre	November
décembre	December

Seasons

printemps	spring
été	summer
automne	autumn
hiver	winter

Directions

nord	north
sud	south
est	east
ouest	west
droite	right
gauche	left

World Wide Web Information

T he Web has become an important resource for travelers, and anyone planning a trip will find a great deal of valuable information here.

The websites listed are all places I've made use of. I have no control, though, over the accuracy or completeness of any websites but my own, and these are presented only as possible additional resources for you to consider. Sites listed here include brief descriptions, available languages, and the URL of each site. Remember, though, that the Web is an evolving place, and websites come and go. If you find a broken link, or discover one you think would be helpful to other readers, please let me know.

Links to all these websites, and changes in them, will be provided in the most important website of all, the *Paris for Families* homepage at:

www.interlinkbooks.com/parisforfamilies.html

We'll begin with the best of general Paris information websites.

General Information

Paris-Tourism (French, English)
The official city of Paris website
http://www.paris-tourism.com/indexf.html

Paris Tourist Office (French, English, German, Spanish, Italian)
http://www.paris.org/OTP/

Paris Pages (French, English)
Huge collection of links on every subject
http://www.paris.org/parisF.html

Paris Convention & Visitors Bureau (French, English)
Lots of business material, but much general information as well
http://www.paris-touristoffice.com/index.html

Smartweb Paris (French, English)
Good general information site
http://www.smartweb.fr/fr/paris/index.html

French Tourist Office official site (French, English)
Includes a section for Paris
http://www.francetourism.com/

Time Out (English)
Big London entertainment magazine's comprehensive guide to Paris
http://www.timeout.com/paris/index.html

Paris Web (French)
Great collection of local information
http://www.paris-web.com/

Interlink Publishing (English)
Great selection of books on Paris, including *The Cafés of Paris, Paris by Bistro,* and *A Traveller's History of Paris*
http://www.interlinkbooks.com

Accommodations

The Web contains far more information about accommodations than any travel book could possibly publish. Remember that companies sometimes make their own properties look more attractive than they warrant, but the amount of information provided is far more than you could get from even the world's greatest travel agent.

Rendez-Vous Parisien (English)
Apartment rentals in central Paris
http://www.ndirect.co.uk/~patoud/index.html

World Wide Travel Exchange (English)
More than 50 apartments in all price ranges; links to
individual owners
http://www.wwte.com/europe/france/paris.htm

Paris Pages hotel links (French, English)
List of 2,000 hotels with reviews. Terrific list, full information
http://www.paris.org/Hotels/

Time Out's accommodation pages (English)
Good reviews of hotels & some apartments
http://www.timeout.com/paris/accom/

Hotels Paris (French, English)
Nice variety of hotels and apartments
http://www.hotelsparis.fr/

Home Rental Services (French, English)
More than 100 apartments
http://www.homerental.fr/

Getting There

More people each year book transportation through sites on the
World Wide Web. Here is a selection of useful addresses.

Internet Travel Network (English)
General travel information from American Express
http://www.itn.com/

Microsoft Expedia (English)
Popular general travel site
http://expedia.msn.com

Air travel services (English)
Airline prices and links
http://www.flifo.com/

Sabre flight booking website (English)
Use the same computer system travel agents use
http://www.travelocity.com

Priceline (English)
Name your own ticket price, but watch restrictions
http://priceline.com

Homepages of world airlines (English and various other languages)
Check prices directly with airlines
http://smilinjack.com/airlines.htm

Rail Europe (English)
Good collection of rail information
http://www.raileurope.com/

European Railway Server (English & others)
Links to most national rail services in Europe
http://mercurio.iet.unipi.it/

SNCF French Railways (French, English)
French national railway system
http://www.sncf.fr/

Paris Airports (French, English)
Up-to-date information about both Roissy-De Gaulle and Orly
http://www.visit-paris.com/airports/

Paris Train Stations (French, English)
Arrivals and departures, directions, and more
http://www.paris.org/Gares/

Paris Traffic Reports (French)
See how bad traffic can be. Includes roadwork delays
http://www.sytadin.tm.fr/index_paris.html

Restaurants

Many of the general websites above have restaurant sections.
The link below includes more restaurants than many sites, and
includes reviews from readers.

Paris Pages Restaurant Guide (French, English)
200+ restaurants, especially in arr. 8, 16 and 17
http://www.paris.org/Restaurants/

Transportation

Here are two great sources for learning about the RATP
system—the Metro, the RER, and the buses.

Official RATP Website (French, English)
Routes, maps, fares, tips. French version more is complete
than English
http://www.ratp.fr/
Paris Transport FAQ (English)
From Germany – many good tips on using the system
http://www.jura.uni-sb.de/~threich/paris/faq.htm

Currency

Confused about money? This page has everything you might want to know about the euro.

Euro Page (English)
Currency conversions, pictures of notes and coins, details
http://freeusers.digibel.be/~gedesmet/euro/euroinde.htm

Media

If you want to live like a local, read what the Parisians read. Great for planning ideas and getting in tune with the city before you leave home.

Metropole Paris (English)
Nice on-line magazine
http://www.metropoleparis.com/

Pariscope (French)
Weekly Paris entertainment magazine
http://www.pariscope.fr/

Media links (French)
Paris newspapers and magazines
http://www.paris-web.com/Presse/

Museums

To find general information about Paris museums, special passes, discounts, and more, try one of these sites.

World Wide Web Information

Paris Pages (French)
Good information on museum and monument admissions and
hours: *http://www.paris.org/Musees/*;
http://www.paris.org/Monuments/

Paris for Kids (French, English)
Assortment of attractions for young people
http://www.visit-paris.com/kids/index.html

Carte Musées et Monuments (French, English)
Official information on the museum pass
http://www.intermusees.com/

Monuments of France (French, English)
Official site for many monuments
http://www.monuments-france.fr/

Paris Attractions

Arc de Triomphe (English)
http://www.franceguideprestige.com/arc.htm

Assemblée Nationale (French)
http://www.assemblee-nationale.fr/
http://www.assemblee-nationale.fr/7/visite/7cfe.htm

Catacombs (French)
http://www.paris-web.com/Insolite/Catacombes/

A virtual walk down the **Champs-Élysées** (French)
http://www.iway.fr/champs-elysees/

Cimetiere du Pere Lachaise (French)
http://gargl.net/lachaise/

Cité des Sciences (French, English, Spanish)
http://www.cite-sciences.fr/

Disneyland Paris (French, English, German, Italian, Spanish, Dutch)
http://www.disneylandparis.com/

Eiffel Tower (French, English)
http://www.tour-eiffel.fr/

Élysées Palais (French)
http://www.chez.com/parisvisite/elysee.html

Ile de la Cité (French)
http://www.chez.com/parisvisite/cite1.htm

Institut du Monde Arabe (French)
http://www.imarabe.org/perm/musee_id.html

Latin Quarter & Left Bank (French)
http://www.parisrivegauche.com/

Montmartre (French, English)
http://www.montmartrenet.com/indexb.html
http://www.chez.com/parisvisite/montmartre.html

Mosquée de Paris (French)
http://www.smartweb.fr/fr/eglise/mosquee/page.htm

Musée du Louvre (French, English, Spanish, Japanese)
http://www.louvre.fr/

World Wide Web Information

Musée d'Orsay (French, English, Spanish)
http://www.musee-orsay.fr

Musée Rodin (French, English)
http://www.musee-rodin.fr/

Musée National d'Art Moderne (French)
http://www.cnac-gp.fr

Musée National d'Histoire Naturelle (French)
http://www.mnhn.fr/

Musée de l'Armée (French, English)
http://www.invalides.org/

Musée Carnavalet (French)
http://www.pariserve.tm.fr/culture/musee/carnavalet.htm

Musée Grévin (French, English)
http://www.musee-grevin.com/

Musée de l'Homme (French)
http://www.culture.fr/culture/nllefce/fr/mh/indexmh.htm

Musée de la Monnaie (French)
http://www.finances.gouv.fr/patrimoine/musee_de_la_monnaie/visite/

Musée de la Préfecture de la Police (English)
http://www.policeguide.com/Paris-Police-Museum.htm

Palais de la Découverte (French)
http://www.palais-decouverte.fr/

Palais du Luxembourg and French Senate (French)
http://www.senat.fr/visite/visit.htm

Parc Astérix (French, English)
http://www.parcasterix.fr/

Parc de la Villette (French, English)
http://www.la-villette.com/

Pompidou Center (French)
http://www.cnac-gp.fr/

St-Germain-des-Pres (French)
http://www.saint-germain-des-pres.com/

The Seine (French)
http://www.smartweb.fr/fr/paris/indexseine.html

La Sorbonne (French)
http://www.sorbonne.fr/

Interlink's Bestselling Travel Publications

The Traveller's History Series

The Traveller's History series is designed for travellers who want more historical background on the country they are visiting than can be found in a tour guide. Each volume offers a complete and authoritative history of the country from the earliest times up to the present day. A Gazetteer cross-referenced to the main text pinpoints the historical importance of sights and towns. Illustrated with maps and line drawings, this literate and lively series makes ideal before-you-go reading, and is just as handy tucked into suitcase or backpack.

A Traveller's History of Australia	$14.95 pb
A Traveller's History of the Caribbean	$14.95 pb
A Traveller's History of Canada	$14.95 pb
A Traveller's History of China	$14.95 pb
A Traveller's History of England	$14.95 pb
A Traveller's History of France	$14.95 pb
A Traveller's History of Greece	$14.95 pb
A Traveller's History of India	$14.95 pb
A Traveller's History of Ireland	$14.95 pb
A Traveller's History of Italy	$14.95 pb
A Traveller's History of Japan	$14.95 pb
A Traveller's History of London	$14.95 pb
A Traveller's History of Mexico	$14.95 pb
A Traveller's History of North Africa	$15.95 pb
A Traveller's History of Paris	$14.95 pb
A Traveller's History of Russia	$14.95 pb
A Traveller's History of Scotland	$14.95 pb
A Traveller's History of Spain	$14.95 pb
A Traveller's History of Turkey	$14.95 pb
A Traveller's History of the U.S.A.	$15.95 pb

The Traveller's Wine Guides

Illustrated with specially commissioned photographs (wine usually seems to be made in attractive surroundings) as well as maps, the books in this series describe the wine-producing regions of each country, recommend itineraries, list wineries, describe the local cuisines, suggest wine bars and restaurants, and provide a mass of practical information—much of which is not readily available elsewhere.

A Traveller's Wine Guide to France	$19.95 pb
A Traveller's Wine Guide to Germany	$17.95 pb
A Traveller's Wine Guide to Italy	$17.95 pb
A Traveller's Wine Guide to Spain	$17.95 pb

The Independent Walker Series

This unique series is designed for visitors who enjoy walking and getting off the beaten track. In addition to their value as general guides, each volume is peerless as a walker's guide, allowing travellers to see all of the great sites, enjoy the incomparable beauty of the countryside, and maintain a high level of physical fitness while travelling through the popular tourist destinations.

Each guide includes:

• Practical information on thirty-five extraordinary short walks (all planned as day hikes and are between 2 and 9 miles), including: how to get there, where to stay, trail distance, walking time, difficulty rating, explicit trail directions and a vivid general description of the trail and local sights.
• Numerous itineraries: The Grand Tour which embraces all thirty-five walks; regional itineraries; and thematic itineraries.
• One planning map for the itineraries and thirty-five detailed trail maps.
• Trail notes broken down into an easy-to-follow checklist format.
• A "Walks-at-a-Glance" section which provides capsule summaries of all the walks.
• Black and white photographs.
• Before-you-go helpful hints.

The Independent Walker's Guide to France	$14.95 pb
The Independent Walker's Guide to Great Britain	$14.95 pb
The Independent Walker's Guide to Italy	$14.95 pb
The Independent Walker's Guide to Ireland	$14.95 pb

Wild Guides

An unrivalled series of illustrated guidebooks to the wild places far from home and work: the long walks, mountain hideaways, woods, moors, sea coasts and remote islands where travellers can still find a refuge from the modern world.

"The Wild Guides will be enjoyed by everyone who hopes to find unspoiled places."

—The Times (London)